Disaster Avoidance

Active Disaster Recovery
For small business

By

Gary Hawkins, Brian Hitchen and Paul Rumsey

Contents

Foreword

It is excellent to see a book specifically for the smaller organisation on disaster avoidance, although equally applicable to the larger organisation.

The authors have considerable experience in disaster avoidance at the practical level and thus their guidance is based on real world experience.

For smaller organisations you probably don't have a Business Continuity Specialist, and may not even have a fulltime IT Specialist and this book is written specifically for the non IT person.

Many smaller organisations never recover from a significant disaster and end up closing down, you don't want to be one of these, so I believe this is essential reading for you.

Thus I strongly recommend you to read this book for the sake of avoiding disaster and thus potentially destroying your organisation.

Bob Harvey
Past President British Computer Society (BCS), the Chartered Institute for IT

Introduction

Who are we?

Gary

Gary has worked in information security for over a decade and combines technical hands-on experience with ethical hacking, architectural advice, and compliance oversight. Cutting his teeth in manufacturing he has focused over the past five years on insurance and financial services, where protection of data assets and systems is more stringently regulated. He spends his free time exploring application and web development in order to better understand how such systems can be broken and subverted.

Brian

Has worked in IT since 1972. He has mainly worked in the UK, with a brief spell in the Middle East working for Saudi Telecom. He worked on large Mainframe computers, on to Mini and Server based computing and on to various personal and portable devices. He worked in a variety of industries, from manufacturing, banking and financial service companies through to consultancies. He spent the last 30 years working in IT Security and for the past 18 has been responsible for running a computer forensics and investigations facility within the scope of his IT Security responsibilities. He is a member of the British Computer Society, a STEM Ambassador and works with his local Cyber Security Cluster to assist small businesses.

Paul

Paul has 27 years of progressive IT experience and has worked for multinationals in the US and more recently in the UK. He has been a professional broadcaster and entrepreneur in the entertainment industry and managed his own companies. With a Senior Management background in Service Delivery, his current work involves creating and heading up an IT Governance team for a leading UK insurer using ITIL best practices as a foundation. He specialises in IT incident and crisis management and always has to take into consideration the companies requirements and balance that with the needs of IT. His tested experiences in California included earthquake business disaster recovery and also hazardous material handling experience. He is a member of the British Computer Society, holds an Honorary Doctorate in Philosophy and a degree in Broadcast/Communications.

The Cover

Thanks to Linda Hitchen for the cover design.

Who is this book for?

This book is aimed at small to medium sized businesses. For the most part these are companies that will not necessarily have a business continuity plan, or the skills to write one. Many of these companies will be relying on IT to assist them but most will not have full-time IT or a Business Continuity Specialist. While many of the drivers for business continuity, disaster recovery and disaster avoidance will come out of IT, it is the whole business that you will need to look at. The aim of this book is to provide you with some of the missing information to help you look at your business as a complete entity.

Why Disaster Avoidance?

There are many good books on the subject of Disaster Recovery (DR) but there are 2 issues with all of the books we have seen.

1) Most are written for larger companies who have a DR department or at least a full-time specialist working on the subject. These books are very valuable to specialists in the field who deal with the various issues on a day-to-day basis and who know how to assess the ever changing risks that the company faces. If your main task is to keep the company running then they may not be as helpful to you as they are to a DR specialist.

2) By focusing on Disaster Recovery, there seems to be a subliminal message that suggests it is somehow acceptable for the disaster to occur so long as you have a plan for recovery. Many small businesses that suffer a large disaster (say a fire) will fail to recover. They will experience such a large scale business interruption that they are unable to continue. Even large businesses will usually suffer a large fall in their income and profits but they may have the resources to continue to trade from other branches or offices. They may have a good track-record and reputation with a large customer base and the resources to recover whereas a smaller company may well fail. We therefore decided to focus on the

12

avoidance of disasters wherever possible. To help you focus on the risks and issues and to see how you can reduce the risks and identify the steps you can take to mitigate the impact of the issues.

How to use this book.

The book is both instructional and a quick reference guide. The 7 sections can be read through in sequence or taken in isolation. Therefore there is some duplication of information to ensure that each section is complete in itself without having to go back and forth to obtain all the information you need. If you find that you are reading material that you have covered earlier, please feel free to skim-read that part but we felt that it was better to repeat some material than to refer you back to an earlier section. This is particularly important to anyone reading this as an e-book, where moving back and forth through the text can be frustrating.

In the following paragraphs we give some examples of active disaster avoidance. We tried to give some examples that would be meaningful to most people but realised that some examples would be better than others, depending upon your particular background. We have therefore given a number of examples but please feel free to skip them once you "have got the message" that some companies have to avoid a disaster. If you are running a small business, you need to be in the avoidance rather than the recovery business if you possibly can.

Key message.

There are many risks that your company faces on a regular basis that you avoid but you probably don't think about in process terms. Let's take a simple example. You have travelled to a new city for a meeting in the morning. You have the evening free and decide to get away from the hotel and have a bite to eat. So you leave the hotel and head into the city centre. After a while you realise that you have wandered into a less-well populated area where there are a few abandoned cars and some of the street lamps don't work. You realise that you are moving into an area that is potentially dangerous, so you turn around and walk back to a find a well-lit, safer street. In the process of doing this you carried out a quick risk assessment and implemented an avoidance plan. This may seem to be just common sense but recognising the risks for your business is a similar process. In the case of your business, this is NOT common sense, you probably need some guidance in order to know how to identify and assess the various risks that you need to avoid and that is what this book is designed to help you do.

Examples of Disaster Avoidance

There are many companies and organisations that have a Disaster Recovery department in place but there are others that can't afford to have a disaster. These companies have decided that the cost of a disaster in terms of money, reputation or public or governmental backlash means that they have to do their utmost to avoid a disaster from happening. For these companies the cost of a failure in their main operations would be very costly so they are able to allocate a large budget to the avoidance of a disaster. These organisations practice Active

Disaster Avoidance and here are some examples of these industries.

The Airline Industry

Within the aircraft industry the emphasis is on avoiding "in-air" problems. They may split their operation into two main parts, the "in-air" operation and the "ground-based" operations. They may decide that a failure of their ticketing system, while they will try to avoid it, is still acceptable from a public perception point of view. Most people will accept a "computer error" when they book a flight without realising that the airliner will be very reliant on computers, their operating systems and the applications that they process while the aircraft is in the air. However, most people will make a distinction between what happens to the clerical side of the business and the in-flight operation. If a haulage company suffers a serious mechanical failure with one of their trucks they may have a vehicle stopped at the side of the road or even an accident but few people would say that they will no longer trust that company to move their goods based on a single event. Yet when there is an aircraft accident, or even a "near miss" as the press likes to call it, the flying public may lose confidence and the value of the company may take a serious hit.

As a result of the need to avoid a disaster in the air, the airline industry has a series of pre-flight checks that every aircraft has to pass before it can take off. In addition, the servicing schedules for the body of the aircraft, the electrical and mechanical components and the engines are very strict and have to be shown to have been adhered to before the aircraft can fly.

The Oil and Gas industries

Oil exploration, production and transportation are extremely hazardous and the potential for a serious accident is ever present. For this reason the industry operates to very strict standards that are designed to prevent accidents from happening. When things do go wrong the consequences are often very serious from environmental damage through to a serious loss of life. We can probably recall the times when things have gone badly wrong and a platform or pipeline has been damaged or destroyed. The industry spends large amounts of money and effort preventing these incidents. There have been a number of incidents that have been widely reported, from the BP spill through to the Exxon Valdez tanker wreck to the Piper Alpha oil platform disaster where there was a large loss of life. While these are very rare incidents the cost to the companies involved can be very high. The Exxon Valdez tanker disaster caused substantial damage to the coastline of Alaska and while the original fine of $5 billion was reduced on appeal by the American Supreme Court to £500 million this is still a sizeable amount of money. Because of the amount of effort that is spent on looking for weak-spots and preventing them from causing an accident, these accidents are very rare.

Chemical Industry

When chemical plants go wrong, the impact can be massive. One of the worst chemical accidents occurred at Bhopal, in India when the American owned Union Carbide Chemical Plant suffered a leak that killed just fewer than 4,000 people and injured over 500,000 more. While the monetary cost to Union Carbide was £407 million at the time (some £907 million in today's money) the result was that they ended up selling the chemical plant. While the environmental cost was large at the time (1984), the cost today would be far higher. Chemical companies have to remain vigilant and a similar accident today would be likely to cost the company tens of billions of dollars.

What does this mean for your business?

We have looked at examples of industry sectors and organisations that have had to work with proactive disaster avoidance at their core. If you are operating a small to medium sized business, you probably do not have the skills within your organisation to implement a comprehensive DR plan and to be able to test this regularly. There is one thing that you do have in common with these larger industry sectors above and that is for any small to medium business, disaster avoidance is the only practical option. If you are small and suffer a large disaster, there is a very good chance that your company will not survive. If you are hit with a massive and lengthy county-wide flood, then there is little you can do about it and your company may well fail. However, there are many small companies that fail because they suffer much smaller incidents that they should have been able to withstand if they had understood the risks that they faced and knew how to mitigate them. The aim of this book is to provide you with some of the answers to questions that you didn't even know you should have asked. If you have started a small company, you already have a great deal of drive and determination to succeed. You are working in a field that you understand and that you have assessed but just as you will have to become a Human Resources expert when you hire your first employee, so you will also have to understand and deal with many issues that are outside of your immediate field of expertise. Just knowing that you need to address a particular issue should give you the power to avoid being taken by surprise later on.

Part 1 – Understanding your business

In order to look for the risks that your business faces it is vital that you understand all of the various processes that are used in your business. You will no doubt be familiar with the processes that you use to earn your income but you also need to list the various support processes such as your accounts, payroll, maintenance programs etc. Any process that is used to keep your company running may be a weak link that is open to failure or attack. You need to identify all of these and list them. At this point we will introduce the Brain Storm as a way of helping to identify any missing process, or later on, a risk that relates to your business.

The Brain-Storm.

You are probably working on and for your business for many hours a week. It may well be that you have been doing this for several years and haven't taken the time to assess your business afresh. Ideally you should read this section and use it to act as a prompt for the various processes that your company uses and later on you can use this to help identify the risks that your company faces.

As well as doing this now, you should pick an easy to remember date (your birthday, or that of your company for example) to take the opportunity to assess your companies processes and its risks. This is particularly important if your company is growing at a steady rate, or if your business is in a market where the processes can become out-dated and the risks it faces can change quickly.

The rules for a brain-storm are quite simple, but you will need to follow them if you are to get the most out of the session. You should ensure that all the people who are to attend are fully briefed and have had a chance to prepare for the session.

1) Tell the people you have invited to the brain-storm what you want to achieve and what you want them to do. It is best if you tell them in advance of the meeting so they can get into the right frame of mind and give them some written examples of what you want to cover.

2) Write the title and a one-line description on the page of a flip-chart pad. This will help focus minds during the meeting. This is not very high-tech but you want to have a record of what everyone has said and they should be able to refer to this during the meeting. There are alternatives to a flip-chart board but whatever you use should be quick to write on and be clear for all to see.

3) Work your way around the group, one at a time asking for a single suggestion from each. At this stage you may need to encourage people to open up but don't press them. If someone wants to pass, that's OK. You will find that some people get into the swing of things quickly and others will need a little time to get going. The point is to get the whole room thinking creatively.

4) Write down ALL the suggestions. At this stage no-one should pass any judgement on what is said, that will come later. This is very important. There are no "silly" suggestions, simply write them down without passing any comment. Next to each, note who made the suggestion. It can be helpful to record the session, so that you can go back to make sure you haven't missed any ideas. If you are working your way around a room and writing quickly, you may find you have trouble reading some of the ideas later, so to be able to check what was said may be of help.

5) Encourage all ideas, the more free-flowing the better. Quantity is good, look for quality later. Remember, before you find your handsome prince, you have to kiss a lot of frogs!

6) Keep going until all ideas have been written down and there are no more suggestions. If you find the ideas are flagging it can be worth taking a short break to let people read what has been written down. This can generate more ideas.

7) Once you are happy that you have all the ideas recorded you can group them into types, so you can discuss them easier. It is easier to take a little time to get them into "themes" than jumping from subject to subject. You may well find that there are several ideas that are in effect the same, that's OK as the aim of the original session was to make sure you had as many ideas as possible. If you now find that three or four people suggested the same idea, it simply means that it is probably an important idea that it is well worth discussing in a little more depth.

8) If you are identifying a series of processes, then you may have enough information at this point. However, if you are using the brain-storm to identify an idea, or a risk then you will need to look at the various ideas that you have generated to see where it fits.

9) Take each of the ideas and talk them through. Now you can ask the original contributor to expand on their idea. Try to be constructive because it is not helpful to put down an idea. If the contributor wants to withdraw the suggestion, that's OK. You will often find that a good brain-storming session results in a number of ideas that are outside the scope of the original session or that no longer seem valid. When that happens it suggests that you have probably got some good ideas to work with.

10) If it is appropriate, and this will be very helpful when you are looking at risks, you can list the refined ideas into 3 groups.

- Those you can tackle NOW
- Those you can tackle LATER
- Those you can't do anything about YET

Now you have your list of risks that you need to consider where each will come from.

The Business Process Map

It may seem obvious but if you don't really understand your business you will find it hard to fully assess the risks that it faces. We need to understand your business in terms of the various processes that it uses and to do this we will use a Business Process Map (BPM). The subject of BPM can be very complex but also extremely beneficial to weed out cumbersome processes that you can improve or even remove. There are many books written on the subject and a number of specialist consultants who can help you look at your processes so you can streamline what you do. We are using the BPM to help us understand what you do so you can identify any risk areas that you can address. Let's therefore look at a simplified process map.

The BPM Symbols

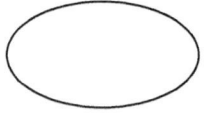 The oval is used to initiate and terminate a process, so you only ever have 2 of these in any one Map.

 The rectangle is used to identify an action and will be the main shape that you use.

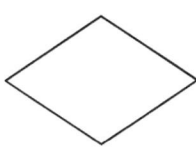 The other shape that you use is the decision and these are almost always used to show when a Yes / No question has been asked.

 Finally we have the direction arrow. This shows the direction of the process and will normally go from top to bottom or left to right.

The High-Level BPM

There are 2 main ways of producing a BPM and these are the high-level map and a detailed map. To start with we will use a high level map of the various processes that your company uses. Both the high-level and the detailed level maps use just 4 symbols that come from a flow-chart template. Many word-processing software packages will let you draw flow-charts and the advantage of using a BPM to show your various processes is the way that you get a high-level view of what you are doing. Some business processes will be very complex and it is easy to get bogged down in the detail, so we will use a high-level view first.

For our example we will look at a fast-food outlet making a simple Pizza. At a high level there are just a few steps.

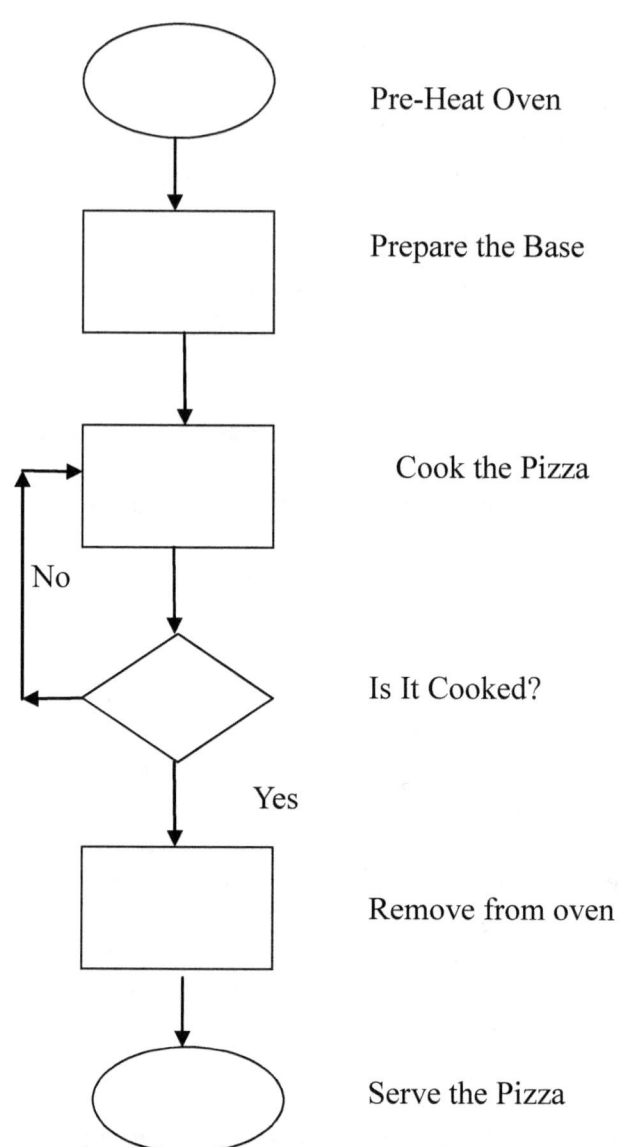

Pre-Heat Oven

Prepare the Base

Cook the Pizza

No

Is It Cooked?

Yes

Remove from oven

Serve the Pizza

A quick look at this will show that it is a simplified process map but if your company has a number of processes, then seeing them at a high level may help to identify any overlapping processes that you can remove or replace with a simpler one.

The Detailed BPM

If you need to go into greater detail than the high-level map gives you, then you can use a detailed map. We will use the example of the Pizza for this.

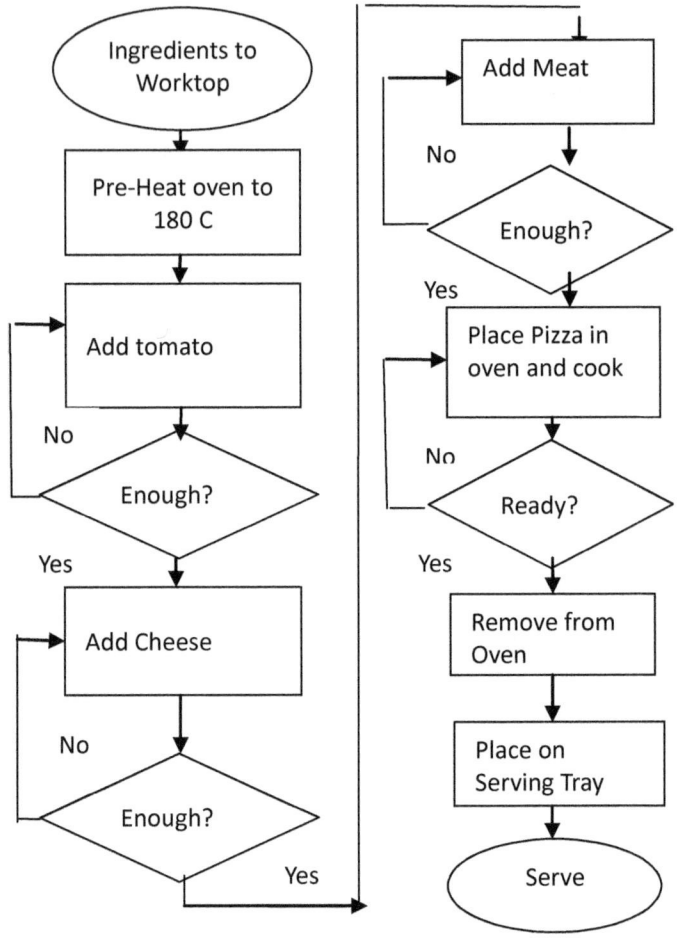

You can see that this is far more detailed than the high

level map that we produced earlier. If you need to look at the processes to identify your risks, then you will need to go into this detail. Of course you can go into more detail still if you find that helpful but it is hard to break down your business processes into their component parts without writing them down or showing them in some sort of flow-chart.

Written Business Processes

You can produce a written list of the various processes if that is better for you and as an example we will look at a taxi company. On the face of it there are just a few processes that would seem to be needed in order to run a taxi company but when you start to list them or draw a chart it soon becomes clear that there are quite a few, so let's take a look at a fairly simple list:

The company will need an admin system that will keep a track of a number of things, for example.

The vehicles
- The age of each vehicle
- The mileage completed
- The number of licensed seats
- The taxi licence number
- The Date of the last MOT
- The cost of insurance
- Details of any insurance claims
- Finance details

- Date of last service

Items that need to be replaced before the next service

Driver Details
- Driver name
- Driver Address
- Driver DOB
- Driver status (employee, self-employed with own taxi, self-employed jockey)
- Driver Company (if they are self employed and use a company name)
- Age of driver
- Any motoring convictions
- Any health issues
- Driver claim history

Account holder details (private and company)
- Account holder name
- Account holder address
- Outstanding balance of accounts
- List of regular trips

List of Garages used (for mechanical repairs, body work, electrical work, tyres and exhausts and fuel)

Outstanding bills for each of the garages

Office equipment (radios, computers, taxi-meters etc.)

Rate tables for regular runs to airports, sea-ports, train stations etc.

Staff rota

Diary of booked trips

So for a fairly straightforward business like running a taxi company you can see that there are a number of business processes involved and quite a lot of valuable data that is being held and some of it is sensitive personal data under the Data Protect Act.

In order to see any risk areas the owner will need to keep track of a number of things and if the administration system is prone to failure or error it can be costly. The company reputation relies on a large number of factors as well as just getting a taxi to take people from A to B. Fully understanding the administration tasks and knowing how many there are that they must keep on top of is important to the company running smoothly.

There are a number of potential risk areas such as where vehicles are kept, the security of the vehicles, the radio equipment and taxi meters inside the vehicles and the security of the data that the company uses. Just by understanding the various processes in detail will help you be able to see if there are any areas that you can look at from an efficiency point of view as well as where you are at risk of a service interruption.

Conclusion

The reason for writing down your business processes, either in word form or as a diagram is so you can quickly see what processes you use and how these processes work. There are a number of ways that you can map your business and the BPM is just one example but it is simple to use and can be very effective at showing how your various processes are made up.

Part 2 – Your IT Systems

Introduction.

The vast majority of small and medium sized businesses use IT as either their main business or to support their business. The rapid growth of the Internet and social media mean that most companies need to be visible on the Internet if they are to thrive. Along with the rapid growth in the use of IT comes a similar growth in criminal activity. We regularly hear about large multinational companies and government sites being targeted by criminals and it is easy to think that the problem of hackers and cyber criminals attacking company networks is one that only large organisations have to worry about.

Is IT core to your business i.e. can your business easily run without IT?

For many companies who face a threat of hacking or data theft, their IT systems are a particular issue. Basically, companies fall into two main categories in terms of their IT systems. There are companies who use IT to help the business run smoothly by taking care of the back-end systems or processes, and there are companies who use IT as their business. Take the example of an estate agent, without their presence on the Internet, they probably wouldn't stay in business very long. Or any of the various comparison sites that only exist in cyber space. These companies are completely dependent upon their smooth and responsive IT systems.

If you only use your IT systems to help support your back-end systems and don't have these computers connected to a network with Internet access, then you can ignore the IT

Specific sections but please bear in mind that you may still have a supplier who processes your company or customer data and uses their IT systems to do so. If this is the case, then please read the sections on assessing a supplier. These will help you assess whether they are processing and storing your data in a secure manner.

In May 2015 Kaspersky (www.kaspersky.com) reported that criminals had been stealing files from small to medium sized companies using a key-logger called "Grabit". The report stated that the criminals had stolen around 10,000 files from companies in Thailand, India and the US. The industry sectors included chemicals, nano-technology, education, agriculture, media and construction. The criminals seem to be moving their attacks from the very large companies who are spending tens or even hundreds of thousands of pounds a year on cyber defence to the smaller companies who don't have the budgets to defend themselves as well as the larger companies. Having said that, many small companies have no defences in place and no way of detecting an attack. Companies who use a hosting service will be better placed to repel an attack but if a criminal gets a key-logger into the network, the outgoing traffic will look valid and so the defences will not stop the data being stolen unless the company takes precautions. So for any small company that has an Internet facing network, they will need to take precautions.

Remember that criminals will aim to exploit the easiest targets. Many small companies have little in the way of cyber defences and so are seen as an easy target. You should also realise the potential value of your data to a criminal. Many companies are storing data that is worth more to a criminal than it is to them. When you use your data, a single customer record may generate revenue of a few pounds, or even a few hundreds of pounds but that same data to a criminal can be sold over and over again and may be worth many hundreds or even thousands of pounds.

There are a number of risks that are particular to IT and you may not realise how these can have an impact on your business unless you have a good understanding of IT. It is important to keep the various risks in proportion. Most companies will run successfully for years without having a fire, break-in or a major act of Cyber criminality but you stand a better chance of avoiding a risk if you understand how it can happen. The following is a list of Cyber threats and how they can impact your business but most companies can reduce these risks by taking some simple steps. We will look at how you can counter many of these risks in Part 6, "What to do", but it is hard to counter a risk that you don't know exists, so we will look at what can go wrong first. We will therefore look at some specific issues now.

Please remember that the following is looking at your systems and facilities from an IT perspective. If the following seems too technical it may be worth speaking to your IT team or your IT supplier. In section 7 (Help) there are a number of companies and organisations who will offer advice and guidance. However, if you don't realise that a DMZ may help protect your network or that a DoS attack can happen, then it is hard to ask for help, so please read the following and seek guidance on any topic that you feel may be an issue and you don't think you have covered.

Network

Almost all computer systems will be configured to use a

network and the network can be a complex design that needs the services of a specialist to design. While it is beyond the scope of this book to try to turn you into a network specialist we do aim to make you aware of areas where you may need to get specialist assistance. Some of the companies and organisations mentioned in Part 7 – Help will be able to assist with general advice and it is worth taking the time to research your needs. However, there are some things that most computer networks will need to have.

Applications

In simple terms we can consider that any application (program) that runs on your computer systems will either process data internally (like a basic accounting system) or will communicate with other computers over the Internet (as in the case of an e-mail system) and some will do both as with an accounts payable system that will calculate the amount of money that is to be paid to your suppliers and then transfer the money over the Internet through your bank. Any information that needs to pass outside of your network should pass through a Firewall.

Firewall(s)

A Firewall acts as a barrier between the outside world and your network or between one part of your network and another. Firewalls range from small pieces of software that will run on your computer alongside other applications (as in the case of all modern Microsoft operating systems) to large specialist computers. All Firewalls are designed to act as a barrier to prevent unauthorised people and services from gaining access to your resources.

Ports

Firewalls contain a series of ports that are designed to allow a particular type of traffic to pass into and out of your systems. An application that needs to talk to the outside world will need to pass information through one or more Firewall ports. Some ports are pre-configured to handle a particular type of data, or traffic and others can be defined by the programmer who wrote the application. Because of the number of possible types of traffic that can be used in a computer system, there are over 65,000 different ports that can be open or closed. When a hacker attacks a network one of the first things they do is to see which ports are open. This tells them 2 things, firstly it indicates how well your Firewalls have been configured and secondly, it lets them see if there are any unusual open ports that they can use. You should close any ports that you do not need to run your operation. This will reduce the risk of being attacked.

Services.

As with open ports, there are a great many services that a standard installation of an operating system will install. All services are a potential back door into your systems, so you should look at the number of services that are running and remove any that you don't need. This will remove potential vulnerabilities but also speed up your systems as they are not running software that you don't use.

Patching.

Whether you use a network or a single computer you should

look at the security patches that the various software manufacturers release and see if you need to install them. Most people are aware that Microsoft release regular patches to reduce or remove security flaws in their operating systems, but all software manufacturers will release patches from time to time. Before you install a patch it is important to conduct some tests to make sure that the patch will not have a negative impact on the rest of your supplications and systems. Your IT department or supplier should review the available patches to see if you need to install them and they are safe.

Hardening.

The process of closing Firewall ports and removing unused services is known as **"Hardening your System"** but unless you also patch your software, you will be reducing the effect of hardening. Hardening your systems and closing the ports that you don't need is not a trivial task but your IT people or supplier should help.

DMZ.

With any network that includes an Internet facing part and has a support or administration portion, there is a need to have a De-Militarised Zone (DMZ). This is where you configure two Firewalls to act as a buffer between one part of your network and another. If you have a web-site and you also have a database that contains customer data, you will almost certainly need to have a DMZ between them to offer protection from attackers. With large networks you will also have zones of trust that show what type of user or traffic you allow to access that part of your network. Most medium to large networks will have a **Red** zone that contains the public facing web-sites and where the users are considered to be "un-trusted" because you don't validate who they are. The network will then have an **Amber** zone where there is some validation but where the Internet users may interact with some backend processes and then you will have a **Green** zone where only fully authenticated users can access your most sensitive applications and data. In between each of these zones there will probably be a pair of Firewalls creating a DMZ, so many networks will have 3 pairs of Firewalls. The precise configuration will depend on the predicted volume of users that the network is designed to cope with and large networks will also use "load-balancing" systems to prevent one part of the network from being overwhelmed with traffic.

IDS / IPS.

It isn't all bad news and you are not completely defenceless while you wait for your systems to be "hacked". Many networks will actively monitor their traffic for malicious activity. These will probably make use of **Intrusion Detection Systems (IDS)** or **Intrusion Prevention Systems (IPS)**. The main difference between the two is that IDS is looking to alert you or your IT people to a suspicious activity and IPS is looking to take some sort of action when it sees "suspicious" activity. There are also an increasing number of hybrid systems that do both functions in a single unit. The main aim of the IPS is to identify malicious traffic and prevent it from getting to the web applications, thus preventing a security breach including or a denial of service.

Hacking

Hackers are in the news from time to time and they are often made to seem like technical super-men. Hackers are, for the most part, criminals. When they are attacking your web-site with your knowledge and permission, as happens with a penetration test, then they are good but another person using the same skills may be trying to steal your data. The thing to remember with hacking is the fact that a hacker who has decided to break into your computer systems may have a great deal of time and money at their disposal but most hackers are simply looking for a soft target. If your defences seem good, most hackers will not bother to attack you. This is the same with domestic burglary; most are committed by thieves who are looking for easy money.

DoS.

Denial of Service (DoS) attacks are designed to prevent your system, usually a web-application, from working and they usually do this by throwing more traffic at your web-site than it is designed to handle. A DoS attack is generally conducted from a single computer. When this happens, the web-site will fail and go off-line so that your legitimate customers will be unable to access your systems. The service interruption that results can be costly but a DoS attack may also be used to mask a hacking attempt.

DDoS.

A more serious attack is the Distributed Denial of Service (DDoS) and this is where a network of computers (usually a network of computers belonging to unsuspecting users or companies have been compromised and put together into a large collection of computers to attack large networks. When you read about an attack on a Government or Military network, this will almost certainly be from a network of computers that are working to form a DDoS. Sometimes it is not a group of compromised computers but an organisation that has called on their followers to attack a single target. There were a number of attacks against large corporate companies, banks and Governments that were organised by "Anonymous" and "LulzSec" and these could be very disruptive.

While a DDoS attack may seem like a simple act of cyber vandalism, hackers will often use such an attack to overwhelm the network defences and gain access while the IT Specialists are looking to get the applications back on-line.

The design of your network will depend on the type of data that you have the volume of traffic that you expect to handle and the type of user you expect to use your site. Some very small companies may have complex networks that are working hard 24 X 7 and where large volumes of traffic are expected; these companies need to protect their networks and systems and may need to allocate a budget to protecting their networks.

Audit Logs.

If you are trading on the Internet, then you should consider using a good level of auditing of your network. The advantage of capturing audit logs is the ability to see if an attacker is returning over time and thus presenting a serious threat to your company. If an attacker is trying to gain access but failing, you should be aware of the fact and see if you can improve your monitoring. If a hacker does manage to gain access to your network, then the ability to look back at the traffic as captured on your audit logs will aid any investigation and help you know when they gained access and how long they were inside your systems.

Infections.

You will have heard terms such as a virus, Trojan or worm but what do they mean for your company? Generally all of the above can be blocked into a group called **Malware**. This is a hybrid word that means **MAL**icious soft**WARE**. Malware comes in a number of forms that can impact you company in different ways. However, Malware needs to be able to get into your network in order to do harm. If your systems have had the latest security patches applied and you run regular anti-virus scans (we will look later at what other measures you may wish to consider) and you never open an attachment in an e-mail or click on an embedded link unless you are expecting it (even if the attachment looks harmless and it has come from a friend), then you are unlikely to be the victim of Malware. But that is like saying that as a pedestrian you will reduce your chances of being hit by a car if you follow the advice in the Highway Code. Reduce, yes but you will not remove the risk all together. So we will look at the main types of Malware.

DDoS and the criminal "consultant".

Your IT systems can come under attack in a variety of ways but one such type of attack involves criminals identifying companies who are extremely reliant on a web-site to run their business, and launching an attack the web-site. There are a number of ways that they can overwhelm the Web-site but once they have generated enough requests to stop the servers from responding the web-site is unavailable. The attack may use a single computer to generate enough traffic to stop the web-site from responding, in which case this is a Denial of Service (DoS) attack. If your systems are more resilient than that, then they can use a network of compromised computers that they control and bring hundreds, or thousands or even millions of computers into a coordinated attack. This is a Distributed Denial of Service (DDoS) attack. There are criminal gangs who spend their time compromising innocent victims and once they have taken over a user's computer (usually because there is a missing patch from the operating system) they will correct the flaw that they used to gain entry and create an account on the system so that they can get back in at any time they wish.

Once the web-site has been taken down, they can contact the victim company and offer their services as "consultants" to end the attack. If the company pays them, then the attack ends. This form of extortion is difficult to address as the criminals are usually operating from a country where there is no extradition treaty with the UK, so their local police are not very interested in the crime. For the criminal's part they simply say that they were monitoring the web-site and noticed that it had been attacked. They have nothing to do with the attack; they simply know how to end it.

Of course, the criminal consultant is just one way that a criminal can attack your company; there are other criminals, political fanatics and vandals who may see you as a legitimate target. Generally, the vandals simply wish to take your web-site off the air or deface it with some obscene message. Generally they will go away once they have gained entry. The political activist is also likely to move on once they have made their point. However, if you find that your web-site has been compromised, you should make sure that they have not left a back-door through which they can gain entry another time.

Key-loggers

These are designed to record what you type. These are often associated with banking Trojans to record banking log-on details and then send these back to the criminals (see Banking Key-Loggers below) by fooling the network into seeing them as an e-mail message going out. They can be used to gain the sign-on details of a senior manager or a system administrator. They can also be used to record (generally small) amounts of high-value data, such as a particular valuable formula. Key-loggers come in two main types. Firstly there is the physical device that needs to be attached to a computer key-board and will record all the key-strokes until it is removed and downloaded or it fills up. The problem with this type of device is that they are very hard to spot remotely by using security monitoring systems but they are also hard to install and maintain, since the criminal will need to have physical access to your computers. The second type of key-logger is the software type. These can be sent in remotely and while these are easier to try to get into your system, they can often be detected remotely by your security systems.

Banking Key-logger.

This is a particular type of malware that is designed to wait for the victim to log onto a particular bank or group of banks and then steal the authentication details (user account and password). Once it has recorded these details, it will usually make use of the normal e-mail channel to send the information back to the criminals. The problem with this type of malware is that it has almost no effect on your systems. It is so specific in what it wants and so selective in the amount of data that it captures that it is hard to notice any impact on your systems. You will only notice the effect on your bank account once the criminals get hold of your details.

Spam.

Spam may seem like a nuisance but it is really big business. It is also illegal to send Spam in most countries, so the criminals who operate in this market will often use compromised computers to send out the Spam. The criminal will be protected from any legal repercussions of having the messages traced back to their computers and while you would not normally be in trouble for falling victim to a criminal, your systems and your network may well suffer performance issues and you will have to pay for the resources that they have used.

Scare-ware.

This is a nasty type of confidence trick. In effect the criminals infect computers with Malware that displays messages on the main screen to say that the computer has been infected with a virus, or that there are illegal images on the computer and the user must buy a security solution from the company and all the user has to do is to click a link in the message in order to purchase the solution. If they do buy the "solution" then the messages will stop for a while but in reality, the "solution" would simply stop the messages from being displayed. This was known as "snake-oil" in the Wild West.

Ransom-ware.

Is a growing threat and this type of software started a few years ago and worked by encrypting the hard-drive and then sending a message to the victim to demand money for the decryption routine. Many of these infections asked for between £100 and £200 and in all cases that we have seen they would deliver the decryption routine. Until you paid the ransom, all of your documents, and photographs were encrypted so you couldn't use them. Because the people who paid had their data restored for them, this went largely under the radar of the authorities. However, there was a problem for the criminals. If you had a good backup routine, you could restore your system to a time before it became infected and simply ignore the demand.

To get around this the criminals started to install the software and this would encrypt the disk but as soon as you turned on the computer, the system decrypted your files, so you didn't know that you had an infection. However, every-time you backed up your system, the backups contained only encrypted data. Once the software had been on your system for 6 months, then the decryption keys would be deleted and you had a computer with data that you couldn't read. Restoring your data from a backup would not work, since these have also been encrypted. The only quick option would be to pay the criminals. Recently there are a growing number of companies that have been infected, so how can you spot the malware? See below for a write up on the various types of backup and how to protect your data...

Remote Access Tools (R.A.T.s).

Malware will often call back to a central point or a "Command and Control" server so that the criminals behind the malware can monitor activity on your computer, issue new instructions, or load new malware.

Backups.

Data.

As we have seen from the Ransom-ware the way that you do your backups is very important to the well-being of your company. Your core operating systems and any bespoke software should be packed up and tested to make sure you can recover your key systems. Then you can backup these and store the backup media (tape, DVD etc.) so that your main systems are secure.

You should also do the same for your web-site. This may be fairly static in terms of how often you change it, so take a separate backup and keep this secure. You now have your key systems and web-site data secure. Look at your other data and see how frequently this changes.

Provided you try to prevent your software from being updated without your knowledge (see white-listing and HDF later on) you should be able to prevent rogue programs from being uploaded but even if this happens, you'll be able to get back to a prior good state.

Software.

You must backup your critical systems and particularly, any special programs that you use to run your business along with any licence or registration details that are needed to install the program(s). These programs should be kept separate from your data and the backups need to be tested periodically to make sure that your recovery process works.

Hardware.

If you have critical hardware, you should either have a backup of it, or a "plan B" for if it becomes unusable for any reason. Suppose you have a critical colour plotter that costs a great deal of money. You probably won't have a spare one but in the event of a mechanical breakdown you should consider talking to your supplier and seeing if there is another business that you can have a mutual arrangement with so that in the event of your machine becoming unavailable for a time, you can share their machine. Clearly the terms of such an arrangement would need to be worked out carefully. An alternative option would be to have an arrangement with the supplier. If you need the equipment in order to run your business you should have a contingency arrangement in place and tested if you possibly can. You should also establish how long you can manage without the equipment and how long it will take to instigate the contingency so that you can be confident of avoiding any interruptions to your business.

Your Web-Site.

Most companies have a web-site and many will use this to directly generate business. You may sell over the Internet or you may use your Web-Site to generate business, as in the case of an on-line supplier. Many small businesses start with a web-site that is hosted by an Internet Service Provider (ISP) before moving to an in-house hosted system as the company grows. There are a number of advantages to using a supplier for hosting, but you need to think about what data and services are available over the Internet. Try to limit your exposure to on-line criminals as much as you can.

If you can separate your web-site from your back-end processes (where you process the customer orders and store the customer account details), then this is safer than having all your processes and data hosted on a single network. You may do this by having two separate networks, as would be the case if you are using the services of a hosting company for your Web-Site. But if you have a single network with your Web-Site in one sector and your back-end data in another, you will probably have an outward facing Firewall to protect you from hackers and Cyber vandals. You will need to keep the Firewall rules up to date and also to report on and investigate any serious unauthorised access attempts. Most Firewall vendors will be able to provide advice and support if this is an area in which you are not confident.

Your Data.

What is the value of your data to you and what is the value of it to a criminal? Look at your data from a criminal's point of view to try to a work out what it is worth and what steps you may be able to take to protect it. We will look at data in a number of different ways throughout the book. The thing to remember with data is the fact that a criminal doesn't "remove" your data as they would with high-value goods or equipment.

When a criminal copies your data, you still have it, so you may not even be aware that you have been the victim of crime, so you need to make sure that you are alerted to any unauthorised access as quickly as possible. You should listen to a complaint about identity theft or fraud from a customer carefully.

Do you send data to a supplier or your staff? If so, how do you protect it while it is out of your direct control and how do you prevent it from being intercepted in transit? Make sure that your staff and suppliers understand the sensitivity and value of any data that they have access to, and make it clear what actions you consider acceptable and unacceptable. Include these details in any employment contract or service agreement if necessary.

Make sure that you and your key suppliers test to make sure that the backup process works. You must be able to restore your data and use it.

Customer and Intellectual Property Data.

If you hold name, address, phone number and date of birth, you are close to having a complete identity for your customers. Never hold more data than you need. If your business needs to know the age of a customer, do you need the complete date of birth, or will the year be good enough? Even better, will an age band (20–25, 26-30 etc.) be sufficient for your needs? The less specific you can make your data, the safer you and your customers will be.

If you hold intellectual property, then look at the way you store it. Is it available to your web-site? Is it available remotely, for example, if you are working from home? Is it stored in clear-text or do you encrypt it? You may not have thought about the IT Security aspects of the data but if it is vital to your business it may well be attractive to criminal's, then you need to make it hard for them to get at. Remember that if someone "steals" your data, it isn't like them stealing your wallet. If a pick-pocket takes your wallet, then as soon as you go to use it, you will know it is gone. If someone takes your data, you still have it they will simply have taken a copy of it. Unless you have good audit or control systems in place you may not be aware that it has been copied.

In the case of intellectual property, this will be a particular problem, since intellectual property tends to be data that is critical to your business and if it has been taken, then your business may be in particular trouble. With customer data, then as soon as a criminal starts to use the data, there is a good chance that you will be made aware of the fact. While this is not good, it does mean that you will probably be made aware of the theft and therefore you can start to investigate the crime. If you lose intellectual property data, then you may not know about it until it is too late to protect your business.

Payments Data.

If you take payments through your web-site, do you store the credit-card or debit-card number? If so and you are a small company, you may need to be registered with the Payment Card Industry and comply with their Data Security Standards (PCI/DSS). The PCI standards for any company that processes or stores credit and debit card data are very prescriptive and the penalties for not being compliant with their requirements are very harsh. Most companies that need to trade over the Internet, even some very large PLCs will make use of a payment provider such as PayPal or World Pay to ensure that they do not store credit or debit cards on their systems. They will simply store a payment reference number that is of no use to a criminal.

Suppliers.

Do your suppliers have any of your data? Later on we will provide a "Supplier Questionnaire" that you can use to assess the security and resilience of your suppliers. Remember that if a supplier loses your key data or intellectual property, it will be your reputation that suffers. Your supplier may lose one customer (you) but you may lose hundreds or thousands. You need to ensure that your suppliers do not risk damaging your reputation or risk losing your intellectual property. To help you do this we have provided a supplier questionnaire in Part 3 and an assessment form in Appendix "B" that you can use to help you assess their security.

You must also keep an eye on critical suppliers to make sure that they can service your needs and that they are not getting into financial trouble. If you have a critical supplier that you are very dependent upon, you should keep an eye on the market to see if you have an alternative supplier should your existing one get into trouble.

Regulators.

While many small businesses struggle with the amount of regulation they have to deal with, this will increase as your company grows. If you have good processes in place when your company is small and you check them regularly, you should avoid having a nasty shock in the future.

The Data Protection Act applies to any company that stores or processes personal data. You will have a responsibility to maintain the data so that it is accurate, relevant to your business, appropriately protected, and processed only for approved purposes. You must be registered with the Information Commissioner's Office (ICO) and in most cases you must provide your data subjects with a full record of what data you hold about them. There are some very limited exceptions to these rules but for almost all companies operating in the UK, if you store or process personal data, you must be registered with the ICO.

The Financial Conduct Authority (FCA) is responsible for controlling companies that deal in the financial services industry. If you are a bank, insurance company, or give advice about savings, finance and investments you will be regulated by the FCA. You will need to take great care with your customer data, and ensure that you comply with any FCA guidelines such as Treating Customers Fairly.

Malware.

Malware comes in a variety of forms. Many people speak of Virus, worm or Trojan and while there are differences in the way they can get in, they all try to compromise your systems for a variety of reasons. For completeness we provide a brief definition:

Virus – like its human counterpart a virus needs "contact" to spread. This is usually by receiving an e-mail and clicking a link or opening an attachment. A **Trojan** is like a virus but it poses as something that is friendly in order to trick you into opening it. An e-mail claiming to be from your bank with a genuine looking link will be a Trojan. Both virus and Trojan need you to do something in order to get the infection but once in, the virus will almost certainly try to use your contact lists to spread further. Trojans are often content to infect your machine but not give the game away by spreading further. The third form of malware is the **worm**. This is a piece of malware that actively hunts for victims by looking for a weakness in your network set-up or in a particular piece of hardware. You don't have to open a worm, or even be aware that you have it. Malware varies in the way that it will infect your computers but can generally be seen in 2 main forms. There is an installed piece of malware that can be removed easily once your anti-virus (AV) system "sees" it. Then there is a root-kit infection. This is malware that infects your computer and then hides. There is an area on all hard-disks that is reserved for the disk manufacturer to use. This is the engineering sector and may not be addressed by you or the operating system. There are some cunning pieces of software that can write themselves to this area and then be immune from the AV system. Other root-kit software will be attached to the very heart of the operating system (the kernel) and monitor what applications you are running. When the AV system starts a scan, there is a second piece of software that will remove the malware, so the AV system can't find it and then re-install it once the scan has completed.

Anti-Virus (AV).

Most companies protect their data with AV systems. While there are regular articles in the press stating that AV is "dead" and the only way to protect your systems is to move to a White-List approach (see below), only a hand-full of companies have done this. There are a growing number of companies that use both AV and White-Listing to protect their systems and data and very few companies would stop running an AV system, even with the way that criminals can fool them.

White-Listing.

A White-Listing system works by blocking any process that it hasn't specifically permitted to run. The idea is simple. If you contract a virus (or Trojan or worm), then the way that these work is to install an executable on your computer that takes control under certain circumstances. If you have a key-logger, then this will record your key-strokes. In almost all cases these nasty pieces of software are programs that run and are designed to capture your sensitive account details (log-on and password) so that a hacker can pose as one of your a system administrator. Key loggers come in 2 main forms. They may be physically attached to a key-board or even to the circuit board inside the key-board or they may be a piece of software that is inserted into your system to record particular key-strokes.

To defeat the hardware key-logger you need to protect your physical environment but to protect your applications you will need to ensure that any software updates are controlled. While a good AV system will recognise a known virus (or key-logger) the executable that is associated with the key-logger may be defeated if you use a white-list approach. While the white-listing systems are generally very good, they can be rather cumbersome to operate, particularly for a small company.

HDF.

Over the years, anti-virus systems have grown in popularity

but as they have done so, criminals have been working hard to bypass them. While AV is still very widely used, and for good reason, some companies have been looking at white-listing and found that the overhead of using this make it very unattractive. An alternative that has been developed at the Royal Holloway University by a company called Abatis is a system called Hard Disk Firewall (HDF) and is designed to prevent any unknown executable from being written to the hard-disk. While this is similar in approach to a white-list it is claimed that it is has a far lower overhead to maintain and run. HDF software is fairly new but it does seem like an interesting development and if you are looking to upgrade your network protection it would be worth talking to both White-List and HDF vendors.

Attack Types.

When an IT network or system comes under attack there are 2 main ways that this can happen. Firstly there is a remote or automated attack and this is where Malware may be used. You may not even be a specific target; the criminals may simply be spreading malware so they can see who is vulnerable. The other type of attack is where a hacker is aiming at getting into your network in order to steal what you have. With either of the above attacks, you may find that you and your staff are getting "**phishing**" e-mails or phone calls. The most common form of attack is the phishing e-mail and this, like the Trojan mentioned above, is designed to trick you into providing information. Generally these e-mails will impersonate a legitimate company or organisation. However, once you have fallen victim to them the information you provide will be used to steal money or data.

The next type of attack is the **spear-phishing** attack. This is aimed at a particular person or group of people. Large PLCs are often the target of spear-phishing campaigns and because the rewards for success are high, the criminals will invest a fair amount of time in getting the e-mail to look convincing, both in terms of content and style. As a general rule, spear-phishing attacks are aimed at high net-worth individuals or companies. If you are running a small company where your product is very valuable, then you will need to be aware of spear-phishing attacks.

Social Media.

Do you use social media such as Facebook, Twitter or Blogs to promote your business? If so, you are part of a growing number of companies who do. If you do use these, then you must control what is said in the name of your company. Whether you do or not, you should monitor these carefully and to see what is being said about your company. If there are negative comments, you need to act quickly to protect your company name and reputation. Clearly, there are some industries that are more susceptible to negative media than others, but whatever your business it is important not to come across as too combative or defensive when responding to a negative comment.

If you don't use these, you should still be aware of what people are saying about your company on these and the growing number of sites where people can post reviews, such as www.tripadvisor.com. You can search for comments about your company and you may need to take action if someone is saying bad things about your company or the service that they have received. Unfortunately, there are a growing number of people who will complain publicly before trying to resolve the issue with the company, or will be very impatient. If they have a genuine complaint, or if you're not sure, it may be best to reply to their comment with an offer to look into the problem if they will contact you. This isn't to say that you must give in to unreasonable demands but you need to try to resolve the issue so they feel their complaint has been taken seriously.

If you feel you have been given a particularly unfair or harsh review, some of these sites will give you an opportunity to reply, or to request evidence of the alleged incident, from the complainant such as proof that they are a genuine customer.

Examples of other sites that ask for customer feedback are www.ebay.com and www.amazon.co.uk where products and service levels are reviewed. If you start to get bad reviews, you should look at your processes and service offerings to see if you are generating unreasonable expectations on the part of your customers.

Penetration Testing.

There are a number of options you can look at to test the security of your web-sites and back-end systems. In simple terms a penetration test (or pen test) is designed to simulate a hack against your network and systems. While there are no formal definitions of a pen test, there are many different forms of attack.

Scripted attack. This is the simplest form of pen test but don't think that it is not effective. A good scripted attack will use a series of pre-written programs or scripts to attack and assess your system for weakness and let you know what you need to do to correct any errors found. One of the more popular is a cloud-based system from Qualys. To use this you simply need to provide the IP address range of your network and enter this as a parameter for it to scan your systems. Many companies use Qualys to help boost their other pen testing processes. While Qualys is simple to set up and use, you do need some experience to understand what it is telling you.

Blind (or unauthenticated) attack. This is where you hire a pen testing company to attack your network from the point of view of a hacker who has no knowledge of your systems. These are often run by consultants using a range of specialist tools that are designed to look for vulnerabilities in your configuration before planning how to attack your systems. There is one company that uses a form of intelligent scan that will initially look for vulnerabilities and then automatically try to exploit them. This is offered by ProCheckUp and is a cost-effective way of checking that the network will withstand a hacker for a reasonable time. Many blind attacks can be completed in around 5 working days, including writing the report, for a simple network up to 2 or 3 weeks for a more complex network running multiple web-sites.

Authenticated attack. The next level of sophistication comes from the consultants that will use a mixture of the blind-attack to check for vulnerabilities but then attack the systems with some form of authentication. If you run a web-site where you allow people to log-on, then an authenticated attack will simulate the situation you would face when a legitimate user of your systems has had their credentials compromised. These attacks will often use several consultants working together for 2 or 3 weeks to attack your network. While this may seem to be expensive, it is far less than the cost of a large fine from the Information Commissioner or from the FCA and these will be far less than a fine from the Payment Card Providers if you were to lose debit or credit-card data.

Physical penetration. Some specialist companies will test your physical security to see if they can gain access to your building and then compromise your systems. If you have high-value intellectual property or valuable data in your offices, then this may well be a worth-while exercise. You may be surprised at the ease with which a skilled operative can gain access to your building but then be equally surprised at the simple measures that can be used to prevent such access. As with all things, if you know where you have a weakness, you can aim to correct it.

If you are holding high value data or IP, as will be the case with a chemical or a drugs company, or in a Lawyer's office, then it may be wise to review your physical security and to have your key offices "swept" for bugs. There are specialist companies such as XIX Group (see Part 7) who will provide these services, and can assist you with reducing these risks.

Part 3 – Assess Your Business IT Systems

Assessing your systems.

Now you have looked at the various categories above you should be able to fill in a detailed security questionnaire. This should be used to help you understand your systems and see where you have any areas that need to be improved, either now or in the future.

The questionnaire should give you pointers that we hope will be helpful in letting you see where there are potential weaknesses. As this is an internal document, please be as honest as possible, even if this gives a low score. This can then be used to help you formulate a plan of action to improve your systems and processes.

Company Review Criteria.

Background.

Data is a vital part of your business and safe keeping of that data is of utmost importance in order to protect financial interests, maintain regulatory compliance, and to protect company brand and reputation.

Prior to using sensitive data for your business you should review your IT systems, policies and procedures to ensure you are adequately securing your data. This form will help you to assess whether you are protecting your data as well as you reasonably can.

The questionnaire should be considered overall with a view to the service that is to be provided, the size and resources of your company, and the criticality of data that you will be handling.

This document is intended to provide guidance on the criteria that you should aim to indicate. The specific level of security that will be considered acceptable may vary depending on the criticality of the data, the nature of your business, and the nature of your IT systems.

The first half of this document provides generic outlines of each section of the questionnaire with descriptions of the intent and ideal responses. The second half of this document provides specific scoring criteria for the security questionnaire.

This questionnaire is not meant to be prescriptive but to be used to aid you in your risk assessment process. Please make any changes you like so long as you are able to use it to help your company assess the IT risks.

Definitions.

- **Supplier:** As defined above, a Supplier is any organisation not part of your company or group of companies that provides a Service to or handles Data belonging to you.
- **Data:** For the purposes of this document, data is considered to be any information pertaining to customers, business or staff, and includes anonymised or generic information as well as specific identifiable information.
- **Service:** A Service provided by a Supplier may or may not involve the transfer, processing, storage or handling of your Data. A service may also be the provision of goods, facilities, skills or knowledge. If the provision of a service is integral to the success or failure of your business then the service provider should be assessed to ensure that you have adequate controls in place.

Organisation.

You should indicate if Data is stored in countries and with companies where appropriate regulations and guidelines are applicable.

Data stored with a cloud service provider where geographic location of the data can-not be clearly stated should consider the reputation and size of the service provider.

- Data to be stored within the UK is preferred
- Data to be stored within the EU is generally acceptable to any regulators.
- Data to be stored within the US is generally acceptable if the company adheres to Safe Harbour framework, otherwise you should be cautious to avoid storing data in a country where there is no commitment to complying with the UK Data Protection Act.
- Data to be stored in any other country should be considered as a possible risk.

You should know if you are required to comply with the requirements of the Payment Card Industry Data Security Standards (PCI/DSS). If you don't handle any payment details, at all, then you can ignore the PCI requirements. If you use a payment provider, such as PayPal or World Pay, then you need to ensure that your IT systems are still PCI compliant. If in doubt, you should speak with your Merchant Provider to be sure.

Security Policy.

Do you have a documented information security policy and management systems in line with external industry recognised standards such as ISO27000? Are these:

- communicated to, understood and accepted by all employees, suppliers, and agents, at time of enrolment and at regular intervals ongoing
- regularly reviewed to be kept relevant with emerging technology and threats
- supported by senior management
- inclusive of incident and change management procedures

You should indicate accountability and segregation of duties for information security.

You should indicate that where a sub-contractor is used in the provision of the Service, or where a sub-contractor is permitted access to your data, that comparative policies are maintained.

Authentication, Access Control, Auditing and Monitoring.

You should indicate that authentication principles are defined appropriate to the systems which they protect and that

- Password length, complexity, history and life span are balanced
- Passwords are stored securely
- Additional authentication is required for administrative or privileged activities
- Authentication failures trigger system reactions such as auditable records or alerts
- Consecutive failed logins result in account lock-out

Supplier should indicate that

- Access to your Data is provided on a need-only basis
- Access permission allocations and revocations are auditable
- Service activity and data access is auditable

Network Access Controls

You should indicate that appropriate network segregation exists and that
- Development, Testing and Production environments are distinct
- Networks and systems used to provide the Service are segregated from other functions
- Intrusion attempts and malicious activity generate system reactions
- Access from an external connection is restricted and auditable
- Use of wireless networking is restricted and auditable

Data Encryption, Internet Facing Web Applications.

You should indicate that network boundaries are protected by firewall appliances or devices with equivalent functionality. You should indicate that web facing applications and interfaces are
- Tested for security vulnerabilities on a regular basis
- Tested for security vulnerabilities following any significant change
- Segregated from internal networks
- Monitored for malicious activity and intrusion attempts

And that they
- Use appropriate data encryption
- Do not transmit data over an unencrypted connection
- Require authentication if appropriate
- Restrict access to only identified sources if appropriate

Server and PC Protection, Physical and Environmental Security.

You should indicate that procedures are defined for
- Patch management and antivirus updates
- Secure disposal of computer equipment, digital storage media, and printed material

You should indicate that networks and systems are protected against
- Fire
- Flood
- Power interruptions
- Unauthorised physical access

You should indicate that secure backup procedures are defined and that data in storage or transit is appropriately encrypted and secured.

Using the questionnaire below, you should aim to score at least 15 in each section, and any section that scores less than 10 likely merits close attention. The same questionnaire can be used to score your own company and to rate the security of your suppliers. You can set a target score for each supplier depending on the importance of the services that they provide to you.

You can download an electronic version of this spreadsheet here www.disaster-avoidance.co.uk. Feel free to alter it and use it for the benefit of your company.

	Organisation, Policies and Procedures	
1	Is there an individual member of the Senior Management Team assigned responsibility for IT Security?	Yes = 2 No = 0
1.1	If yes then make a note of their name, title and contact number details	N/A
1.2	Number of IT Staff employed within the organisation	N/A
1.3	Number of IT Security Staff	Two or more = 2 One = 1 Zero = 0
1.4	What are their roles and responsibilities?	N/A
2	Which Countries outside the EU will hold your data?	UK only = 4 EU = 3 US (with Safe Harbour) = 1 Otherwise = 0
2.1	If you are processing payment details for your company or customers:	
2.2	Has your company been certified PCI Compliant?	Yes or Not Applicable = 4 No = 0
2.3	If you are working to gain PCI compliance, what is the time-frame?	0-6 months = 2 6-12 months = 1 Otherwise = 0
3	Do you have any documented security related Policy / Standards which are relevant to this venture? i.e. IT Security Policy Laptop/Mobile Device/BYOD Policy	Scale of 0 to 4 based on detail of policies
3.1	If yes, are these documents base on any standard? (e.g. BS7799).If so	Standard Accredited = 4

66

	please provide details of which standard(s).	Based on Standards = 2 No = 0
3.2	Please detail any Information Security weaknesses you are aware of in your installation, together with actions being taken to address these	N/A

	Authentication	
4.1	Do you use user IDs and passwords to authenticate logons?	Yes = 2 No = 0
4.1.1	If No, how do you audit and monitor the use of your systems? Please skip to section 6 – Access Controls	Scale of 0 to 2 based on solution
4.2	Do you supply one user account per member of staff that uses your system?	Yes = 2 No = 0
4.3	Do you enforce minimum password standards?	Yes = 2 No = 0
4.3.1	What is the minimum password length? (for example: 8 characters)	Set = 1 Otherwise = 0
4.3.2	What is the minimum password complexity? (for example: upper case, lower case, non alpha)	Set = 1 Otherwise = 0
4.3.3	After what period is a password change forced? (for example: 90 days)	Set at 90 days or less = 1 Not set, or over 90 days = 0
4.3.4	What is the minimum password lifetime? (for example: 24 hours)	Set = 1 Otherwise = 0
4.4	Do you use a password history	Yes = 1

	mechanism to prevent the re-use of recently used passwords, and if so how many previous passwords are retained?	No = 0
4.5	Is the password database hashed or encrypted?	Hashed = 3 Encrypted = 1 Neither = 0
4.6	How many consecutive incorrect password attempts are allowed before a user is locked out?	Set at 10 or less = 1 Otherwise = 0
4.6.1	How long is an account locked out for?	30 minutes or more = 1 Otherwise = 0
4.6.2	How are password resets or account lock outs managed?	Administrator or Management = 1 Otherwise = 0
4.7	Are secondary secrets, tokens, PINs, or biometrics etc. deployed to provide additional security, for any part of the network or other computer system? If so please provide details	Scale 0 to 3 based on provision of services and security mitigations

5	**Access Controls**	
5.1.1	Are administrative privileges controlled, and only allocated as specifically required?	Yes = 3 No = 0
5.2	Is there a defined process for granting, managing, and revoking access to data?	Yes = 3 No = 0
5.2.1	Is access provided on a strict needs-only basis?	Yes = 4 No = 0
5.2.2	Is a list of users maintained?	Yes = 3 No = 0
5.2.3	Are inactive users removed from the	Yes = 3

	system?	No = 0
5.3	Are users with access to data made aware of its value to ensure that all relevant security controls are adhered to?	Yes = 4 No = 0

	Network Access Controls	
6.1	Are your internal servers and PCs separated from the web and any other external networks, by firewalls or other means?	Yes = 4 No = 0
6.2	Is there a defined process for responding to security incidents?	Yes = 3 No = 0
6.3	Is there a defined process for making changes to your networks and computer systems?	Yes = 3 No = 0
6.4	Do you display a notice prior to logon to indicate that your systems must only be used by authorised personnel?	Yes = 2 No = 0
6.5	If 'Yes' to any of the following four questions please include an outline of the third party and the relationship/access/data/etc.	
6.5.1	Does any third party have access to any part of your network, either directly or indirectly (in-house agents, web VPN or other means)?	No = 3 Yes = 0
6.5.2	Does any third party have your data passed to them by you?	No = 3 Yes = 0
6.5.3	Are you dependent on any third party in order to provide services to your company or group of companies?	No = 3 Yes = 0
6.6	If 'Yes' to any part of 6.5, what measures have you taken to verify their security?	Scale of 0 to 3 based on extend of

		measures defined

7	**Data Encryption**	
7.1	What encryption methods are used to protect data in (digital) transit?	Scale of 0 to 4 based on encryption level
7.1.1	What encryption methods are used to protect data in (digital) storage?	Scale of 0 to 4 based on encryption level
7.1.2	Are encryption keys/passphrases changed at regular intervals?	Yes = 2 No = 0
7.1.3	Do you have a defined data retention and deletion policy?	Yes = 3 No = 0
7.2	Are Intrusion Detection Systems (IDS) or Intrusion Prevention Systems (IDP) used?	Yes = 3 No = 0
7.2.1	If yes, how often is the rule base and alerts reviewed?	Weekly = 2 Monthly = 1 Otherwise = 0
7.3	Is wireless networking used?	No = 2 Only for isolated guest/web access = 1 Yes = 0
7.3.1	If yes, please give details including where wireless access points are located and what encryption and access control are used	Scale of 0 to 2 based on security and access controls

Computer Protection, Auditing and Monitoring

Are all systems protected by Anti-Virus?

Are AV signatures updated at least daily?

Do you use application white-listing?

Are patches applied to the operating system and applications for all systems?

Are patches applied at least monthly?

- Access management

- Policy monitoring

- Real time security monitoring

Are audit logs maintained and reviewed?

If yes are they maintained for at least 6 months and reviewed at least weekly?

Are audit logs kept securely to ensure that records cannot be altered?

	Internet Facing Web Sites (and Web Applications)	
10.1	Is the web site protected by a Firewall?	Yes = 4 No = 0
10.1.1	Is the web site frontend separated from any data backend, or other internal network areas?	Yes = 3 No = 0

10.1.2	Is the web site protected by IDS/IPS/WAF or any other advanced security?	Yes = 3 No = 0
10.2	Do you conduct regular vulnerability scans at least quarterly?	Yes = 2 No = 0
10.3	Do you conduct regular penetration tests at least annually? (tests should include authenticated sessions if applicable, and follow OWASP or similar industry methodologies)	Yes = 2 No = 0
10.4	Will your data be accessible through the website?	No = 3 Yes = 0
10.5	Does any sensitive area of the web site enforce strong encryption?	Yes or Not Applicable = 3 No = 0

	Physical and Environmental Security	
11.1	Is computer hardware (servers, workstations, firewalls, routers, etc) protected for the following?	
11.1.1	- Secured physical access	Yes = 2 No = 0
11.1.2	Is physical access logged, retaining date, time and personnel data?	Yes = 2 No = 0
11.1.3	- Loss of power (i.e. by a UPS System)	Yes = 2 No = 0
11.1.4	- Fire	Yes = 2 No = 0
11.1.5	- Flood	Yes = 2 No = 0
11.2	Is data protected against loss or corruption by regular backups being taken and stored separately from production data?	Yes = 2 No = 0
11.3	What recovery arrangements are in place in the event of your IT network?	Managed Process = 2

		Otherwise = 0
11.3.1	How frequently are these tested?	Annual or more frequent = 2 Otherwise = 0
11.4	Are formal agreements in place to ensure service availability?	Yes = 2 No = 0
11.5	Please describe the policy in place to securely destroy confidential data including electronic, paper based and removable media.	Managed Process = 2 Otherwise = 0

Reviewing the form.

The form above is used to assess your company and later on to assess the security of your main or key suppliers. On the form there are scores against each question and these will vary depending upon the answer that had been provided.

To understand the impact of the scores, please see Appendix B where there is an explanation of the scoring process and what this will mean for a number of different sized companies.

Part 4 - Risk Assessment.

You have looked at the various processes that are involved in your business in Part 1 and looked in depth at your IT systems in Part 2. It is now time to build a risk assessment from this information and go on to build a risk matrix that will allow you to quantify the main risks that you face and get them into a priority order so you know what to address first. Now that you have looked at your business in detail we will recap the main risks to ensure that you haven't missed any important ones. To do this we will split the risks into 2 main categories, Direct Risks and Indirect Risks and then use these to build a risk matrix.

While we will use this section to recap some of the risks that you have already looked at, there may be some that you realise you had discounted before but that they may have an impact on your business. Please feel free to use the first part of this as much as you feel you need and to skim-read any areas that you feel you have covered already. It is important that you build your risk matrix with care as this will allow you to assign priorities to the work that you need to do. Please remember that some risks may be very short-lived, such as a general power failure in a large town or city but the same risk in an isolated rural area could be caused by a power-line being damaged and this could impact your business for several days. Only you will know your business and only you can decide which risks you need to actively avoid and which you can live with. We have given some examples of risks for you to consider.

Direct Risks:

Natural Disasters:

Floods.

These can be from a variety of sources such as:
   A river overflowing its banks
   Flash-flood due to a severe storm
   Tidal flood
   Man-made due to a large water-main bursting

Land-Slide.

Sink-Hole.
Caused by the subsidence of mine-workings or caves, or a geological failure.

Drought.

While droughts are not common in the UK, if you are in an industry that relies on a steady supply of water, then you may need to take this into account. As we experience more extreme weather events, there will be more occasions when we suffer water shortages, so be aware that some industries (brewing, vineyards, garden centres, farming, even fishing and recreational boating) may suffer losses due to drought.

Storms.

As well as the obvious danger of flash-floods caused by a severe storm, there is a danger of disruption and damage caused by high-winds bringing down power-lines, trees and damaging high man-made structures. In winter you can have extreme weather events such as hail and snow.

Pandemic.

The danger of a pandemic can be felt in a number of industries that rely on selling directly to the public, or to companies that sell to companies that rely on sales to the public. If you sell a product to a supermarket that is sold to the public, then you may suffer a down-turn in the event of a pandemic, even if you and your staff are not directly affected. As part of your pandemic planning you should look at ways of allowing your staff to work from home if that is practical. This would be beneficial in the event of a weather related event as flooding and travel disruption due to storm damage as well as an outbreak of bird-flu.

Legal.

Contractual disputes

These can be with your suppliers or customers and even court cases.

Regulatory change.

Changes to regulations that you have to work within can have a large impact on some businesses. Changes to the way that the Financial Conduct Authority operates as well as changes to the Data Protection Act, Consumer Rights, and the Payment Card Industry standards and many other areas that you will need to keep a close eye on. Fortunately there are many good specialist publications, both on-line and in print that you can use to give you advanced warning of what may be coming your way.

Transport.

There may be risks coming from your use of the road, rail, air, ferry and general shipping networks that you need to be aware of. These risks can be you and your staff use of the roads and rail networks for commuting to and from work but also your supplies of raw materials, the delivery of your finished goods as well as the delivery of supporting materials, such as heating oil or gas or even food if you are large enough to have a staff canteen.

Technology.

There are some overlaps in the risks that you face from criminals and these are covered in the Security section but there are other issues that can interrupt your operations. You need to be aware of failures of:

Broadband
Power
General Hardware (Laptop, desktop, tablet etc)
Specialist Hardware (That you can't just buy from a computer store)
Operating System (this may be caused by a large-scale virus attack using a recently discovered system bug)
Specialist Software – This may be used for the production of your goods or service or to operate machinery. The point with specialist software is the need for specialist support that   you can't just obtain on the high street.
DoS

DDoS
3G or 4G network
Land Line

Government Changes.

This may be a change of government where the incoming regime has different priorities from the previous administration, or where the government changes its mind about what is acceptable. This may be caused by a public outcry that causes the politicians to attack your industry or to remove support that was previously there. Think about companies that were offering pay-day loans in a market that the high-street banks didn't cater for. This market grew and other lenders started to see the potential for profit until there were a growing number of lenders with increasingly aggressive debt recovery methods until there was a public outcry against the whole industry.

Environmental Change.

Will a change to the environment cause you to have short-term or long term problems with your components, business model or method of distribution?

Health and Safety.

Will a change to the health and safety culture or law cause you additional expense or even have to change the way you operate? Obviously if you operate in an area where you have to provide your staff with high-visibility clothing, then you will have to purchase it but if there is a change in the pipeline that you can see coming, then you may see a problem on the horizon that you will need to allow for. Generally, health and safety laws are slow to be introduced but once they are on the agenda, they rarely go away.

Your Property.

Risks to your property come from a variety of sources and some of them are not directly under your control but you still need to be aware of the risks. Examples are:

Natural disasters – Such as a flood or land-slide
Water damage – From a burst pipe or other plumbing failure, or storm damage to a roof or   window
Local power failure – This is a failure to your office rather than a more wide-spread power   outage.
Criminal Act – This could be vandalism against your property or theft of your property etc.

Security.

Some of these items will be listed under other headings but the aim of this is to provide a check-list

What are the risks from criminals?

Who would want to target your company? If you run a small tyre-replacement company, you are unlikely to invoke the attention of a rogue Nation State, such as China or North Korea, but if you are developing new drugs that have cost a great deal of time and money to research, you may find that you are being a target for a variety of competitors, including companies that have the backing of a Nation State.

The risks that criminals pose will vary depending upon the type of business that you run. Some of the risks will be well known by you, for example, if you make and sell jewellery from a shop, then you face the usual criminal activity of robbery of your stock as well as theft of the precious metal and gem-stones that you hold in stock. However, if you sell on-line, can a hacker gain access to your web-site and amend the price of your goods? Can a criminal create a false invoice to steal your goods or money?

Criminals will invest a great deal of time, effort and resources if the rewards are sufficient, as demonstrated by the safety deposit box heist of Hatton Garden during the Spring of 2015. While entrusting your stock to a repository might provide a higher degree of security than you could establish and maintain yourself it might also make your stock part of a larger target. As with most decisions relating to security this is one of finding the balance that's right for you.

Would a large-scale distributed denial of service that prevented your customers from accessing your web-site cost you either money or reputation? Would you be willing to pay a "consultant" who offered to stop the attack? Criminals pose risks to your IT systems and these will be dealt with in Part 2 but for now you need to think about the general risks that criminals pose to you and your business.

Is your stock valuable?

If you deal with high-value stock, like a jeweller, then you will know that you need to take precautions with the location of the stock and you will need a good stock-control system. There are other, less obvious risks that can emerge. A few years ago the price of scrap aluminium rose dramatically and pubs and breweries found that the empty bear-kegs became a target for thieves who wanted to sell them for scrap. Both businesses knew that they had to secure the full kegs but the empty kegs were often kept in the equivalent of large sheds with no security and were an easy target for criminals.

The cost of various components can rise and fall. When the price of red diesel rose, there was a theft of heating oil from rural properties. It wasn't easy to secure some of the larger oil storage systems but you need to remain aware of the risks to your stock, computers, vehicles etc. as they rise and fall. Likewise the value may fall so it is important to review your security controls from time to time to ensure that any investment or recurring costs are still worthwhile and providing a feasible return.

Physical Security.

What level of physical security do you need? You will need to look at the location of your business, the profile of your company (do thieves think you have more than you do?) and the value of any stock that you store. Bear in mind that if you hold particularly valuable data, then a criminal may wish to break into your office in order to connect a computer to your network from the inside. It May be easier to get inside your Firewall than to hack through it. A criminal may also want to gain access to your computers in order to attach a key-logger. This may provide them with valuable user account and password details. There have been cases of criminals getting a job as a cleaner in order to gain access to an office. Only you will know the value of what you have within your IT systems or any stock that you hold, but don't assume that a criminal will need to force open a door in order to gain access to your building.

Many small businesses will need to keep their overheads low and therefore look at renting office space in out of the way locations. While this can help get your business off the ground, you need to be aware of the risks of working in an out of the way office. A ringing burglar alarm may not be heard and if this is the case a burglar is likely to know this. There are many cheap ways of having a burglar alarm connected to a web-cam and able to alert you in teal-time. If you are able to log-on to your CCTV system and have a virtual look around, you may get the benefits of a monitored alarm at a low cost. While many CCTV systems are cheap and easy to install you will need to comply with the CCTV regulations and you can find all you need to know at the Information Commissioner's Office web-site www.ico.org.uk.

Social Engineering.

This is a large subject and the purpose of Social Engineering is to extract information, usually about a person (not always the person that is being contacted) and to use that information to gain an advantage, often criminal. The thing to remember with a skilled Social Engineer is that they do not need to gather very much information in a single phone call or e-mail. They can be quite patient and use a series of contacts to gain the information they want. There are a number of ways that a Social Engineer will try to gain information. Let's take a simple example.

Pete wants to gain access to a company in order to access their customer data. He can hack in from the outside or he can try to gain access to the building, OR he can try to infiltrate the IT systems of a supplier who holds the data he wants. He decides to target the supplier. He knows several things about the target. Firstly, they are a medium sized company with a small IT Department (generally these techniques are much harder to use on a very small company because everyone in the company knows everyone else. Having said that, it is not unknown for a small company, holding very sensitive data to fall victim to a Social Engineer). The company has data that is very valuable to Pete but not generally seen as such on the open market or to the victim company. After performing a number of searches using a variety of search engines he knows that his main target (Bill-IT Systems) uses an outsourced IT supplier (Supplier-1) for their IT systems. Bill-IT Systems uses a specialist supplier (Marketing.COM) to generate marketing leads from a data file that they send them. Pete also discovers that Bill-IT Systems is having their main IT system upgraded by an outsourced IT supplier.

Pete logs on to a number of professional and social media sites, such as Linkedin and looks for names of employees of Bill-IT Systems and Marketing.COM. He finds the Help-desk manager for Marketing.COM and the name of the Head of Program Management in Bill-IT Systems. He sends blank Spam messages to several people in both Bill-IT Systems and Marketing.COM to find the format of the e-mail messages. He uses first-name dot last – name at Bill-IT Systems dot com. He uses first initial and last-name without any gaps or punctuation. He uses the first initial dot last-name and soon finds that all the messages receive a "Delivery Failure" for all but the first-name dot last-name format. So now he knows the format of the e-mails. So he sends Spam to the names that he knows work there and gets an out of office message from Susan Clampit, the Help Desk Manager.

He calls the Help Desk and asks for Susan. When he is told that she is not there he explains that he has been asked to look into some performance issues with the new IT system. "Is this about Project Skylight?"

"Yes, I understand there have been a few issues with it."

"Yes, that's right, how can I help?" From the Help Desk operative.

"I need to run some network checks to see where the bottleneck is, so can you give me a couple of users who have been complaining so I can see if I can sort this out?"

From here he gets the name of 2 users, Pete in Accounts and Jane in HR and the Help desk incident numbers for their issues. Then he calls them with the reference number and arranges to come in the next day to run some tests over the lunch period. He is offered a visitor's space. So he then gets back on the Internet and finds the web-site for the outsourced supplier and also of the telecoms company that Marketing.COM uses. From these he creates some fake employee ID cards, making sure he is shown as a contractor (in case they try to call him at the outsourced company and find he isn't listed.) and the next day he visits Marketing.COM and meets Pete who allows him to connect his laptop into their network and now that he is inside their network, their expensive Firewalls, and Intrusion Detection Systems don't see anything wrong with his connection. He is able to look for the data he needs and download it directly to his laptop. After which he leaves with the promise that he will see if he can find the cause of the response issues.

In the course of this example, no-one gave out very much information yet with some targeted searches and a few phone calls he was able to get inside the company and connect his laptop to their corporate network. The key point here is that he didn't even have to hack into the main company (Bill-IT Systems) in order to get at their data because the file was also with Marketing.COM and it wasn't a particularly sensitive file in their opinion.

Phishing.

This is where a criminal sends in an e-mail that looks plausible and seeks information. Phishing e-mails are general and this is often the give-away. If you get a message from your bank saying Dear Customer, you are almost certainly looking at a Phishing message.

Spear Phishing.

These are harder to spot as they are targeted to the intended victim. The sender will have done some basic research on you and will include some seemingly good evidence that they are legitimate. The nature of a Spear Phishing message means that it will almost certainly be looking for information about you. It may "Need to confirm some details" and provide you with some information in order to get additional facts.

It is important to remember that almost every facet of an e-mail can be faked, in particular the sender's e-mail address and any links in the e-mail. If you're not expecting an e-mail, or if it looks somehow different to previous e-mails, or if it's asking you to do something out of character then think twice before reacting. The e-mail might look like it's from someone you know but is the signature or greeting different, is the language used unusual, is the font not typical?

Perhaps call the apparent sender to make sure the e-mail actually came from them, but use contact details that you know are correct rather than rely on details from the e-mail. If the e-mail asks you to click a link then hover the curser over the link first to see where the link actually points. If the e-mail has an attachment then double check the file type, remembering that the icon might be fake, and be wary of any warnings of macros or scripts if you do open an attachment.

Is your stock volatile?

Do you hold stock that is subject to seasonal variation as would be the case with a clothing supplier? Or subject to fashion, again clothing would be in this category but so would many sellers of technology or even things like sporting goods that can be in and out of demand depending on the weather. These companies need to keep a close eye on the variable factors that can result in them holding stock that is no longer desirable and be aware of the cost implications.

Do you hold high-value data?

There are many companies that store data that is worth more to a criminal than it is to them. You have to know the value of your data (more of this in Part 2) if you are to protect it from criminals.

Do you hold high-value intellectual property (IP)? If you are in the chemical research industry or energy exploration for example, you may well be holding very valuable research data from time to time. Other industries will hold valuable intellectual property that could cripple their company if it was lost or became available to a competitor. Criminals may hack into your network or systems or even gain physical access (as in the example above) to your offices in order to collect your data. They may even try to gain access at a low-risk time (when there is nothing of particular value) so they can install key-logging software or targeted Malware so they can let this wait for your high-value data later on.

What are the risks from competitors?

Could a competitor wish to see you out of business? This is obviously more than the day-to-day competitive rivalry that companies have to live with. If you have a competitor that is suffering as a result of your more successful business, you need to be aware of this and take precautions. Possible for a short time, but still, without knowing that you are at risk, you probably wouldn't try to counter the threat.

What are the risks from customers?

Do you have enough, do they pay on time and are they financially secure? Some small businesses supply a very small (sometimes just one) customer. This can be true in the case of food producers who supply a single supermarket chain. While they continue to grow, there is a danger that the company becomes completely dependent on the one customer and if there is a down-turn in the fortunes of the customer, then their relationship with you, as their supplier may suffer. If you are in such a position, you need to be aware of their fortunes. Pay attention to the business press and see what the City thinks about them. Some niche suppliers may find a large outlet very tempting. The outlet may offer growth potential without the need to constantly market your goods. If this is you, you need to be aware of the risk as well as the benefit and include these in your risk evaluation.

Some customers may be vulnerable to a change in market conditions that are outside of their control. As an example, if you are supplying a large energy company, they may find that they are the focus of a competition enquiry that hits their share-price and knocks the public acceptance of them. Could this have an impact on your business? Keep an eye on your key customers to ensure that they remain stable and viable.

Theft
Fraud
Loss of or corruption of your intellectual property
Loss of or corruption of your customer data
Malicious Business disruption – This may be from a variety of sources such as: Hacking of your IT systems to interrupt your business
DoS or DDoS
Civil Unrest
Anti-Social Behaviour -

Economic and Financial
Interest Rate Rise
Cash-flow problems
Severe bad debt
Economic crime – In particular against your bank account such as having a false direct debit set up to take money from your bank account.

Staff.

Staff issues can be very serious to a small company with a

small work-force. On the other hand, numerous studies have shown that people working for small companies tend to feel a higher degree of loyalty than would be the case in a large organisation. However, there are risks that you need to be aware of and plan for.

Key Staff Leave / become sick or have an accident – Staff turnover is a fact of life but if   your business is very reliant on a key member of staff then you should plan to cross-train so   that you have some backup. This can be a particular problem if you run a company that only   has a hand-full of staff. While there may be little you can do if you have just one or two   members of staff you need to remain aware as your company grows and try to have staff cross-train as soon as they can.

What are the risks from disgruntled or ex-employees?

Do any of your ex-employees bear you a grudge that they are likely to act on? You may have had a bad parting with an employee that you have had to dismiss but often these angry outbursts will fade within a couple of days. You need to think about any-one who is more of a real threat. Is there an ex-employee who really wants to see you or your business fail? If so, what could they do to gain revenge? If you have an on-line presence and you feel they may be in a position to harm your reputation, then you must be aware of this in your risk assessments and try to plan accordingly.

There are some Web-Sites that are used by employees to comment on the working environment and the management of their companies. These are used by both current and former employees and may say some damaging things about your company. While anyone can build their own Web-Site called xxx-sucks where xxx is the name of your company, there are Web-Sites such as www.glassdoor.co.uk that encourage current and former employees to comment on the facilities and working conditions in companies. It is wise to search for your company name and also to check out www.glassdoor.co.uk to see what your staff thinks about your company and the management style used.

Suppliers.

Key Suppliers – As a small business you may have some key suppliers that you rely on. Be aware that they may be far more valuable to you than you are to them. They may be supporting your business but they may need to supply a much larger customer and if that happens, will your supplies be at risk? What would you do if your key supplier were to fail?

Price Hike – If you have key supplies of raw material, is this subject to large price fluctuations?

Market Trends.

Is your business in a market that is subject to large swings in fashion, or seasonal trends? If so, you will need to keep a close eye on the factors that have an impact on your business and consider these to be high priority risk areas.

You will also need to watch your main competitors in case you get dragged into a price-war. Clearly this type of risk would not be the normal day to day competition but could result from a competitor being taken over and having a large cash injection for example.

Utilities and Services.

With these risks we are looking at a much larger event than a small power-failure for example, so these will only come into play if they are long-running and can have a large impact on your business. Be aware that if your business is in a remote location, you may be more vulnerable to power failure than if you are located in a larger community, such as a town, city or a large industrial estate.

Power (electrical, gas and diesel)
Phone system
Mobile (cellular) phone signal
Water
Waste water
Fuel

Indirect Risks.

This is really looking at the "laws of unexpected consequences" and covers things like the ability of your suppliers to cope with a rapid growth in your business. What if there was a general shortage of your raw materials, would that cause you a problem? If there were a particularly harsh winter, would that impact on your ability to do business and if your customers were impacted, could that feed through to you?

Clearly there are some risks that you simply can't deal with in process terms such as a very wide-spread event of the sort that wiped out the Dinosaurs but you can be aware of the lesser events and plan to avoid them where you can.

The Risk Matrix.

Now that you have a list of risks that you wish to consider, you need to calculate a priority list.

There are 2 parts to calculating a risk matrix. For each of the risks you are looking at make a note of the value of the Likelihood.

What is the likelihood of a risk happening?

4	Very Likely
3	Likely
2	Unlikely
1	Very Unlikely

You now need to add a value for the consequences of a particular risk happening next to the value for the likelihood. Like this:

4	Severe
3	High
2	Moderate
1	Low

Now you need to multiply the 2 numbers together to produce a priority order, so you get Likelihood X Impact and this will result in another number:

13 – 16	Priority 1	Review now
9 – 12	Priority 2	Review within 3 months
5 - 8	Priority 3	Review within 12 months
1 – 4	Priority 4	No Action

Part 5 – Supplier Reviews

Be aware of supplier risks.

Risks can evolve slowly, say as you become more successful but other risks can seem to come out of nowhere. Brian once worked for a company that was owned by a large parent company. The parent company took over another firm that had a relationship with an animal testing laboratory. Suddenly, the smaller subsidiary became a target for animal rights campaigners, even though the take-over and the relationship with the animal testing laboratory was completely out of their control.

The company had to mount a PR campaign to assure their customers that they had not been involved in the decision to buy the new company and had no connection with animal testing. This situation was resolved quickly because the risk was spotted quickly and acted upon.

You own your data and you are responsible for the security of it, even when you have passed it to a supplier to process it for you. It therefore stands to reason that you should have the right to check the security of any supplier that has been entrusted with your data.

You should use the form that was printed in Part 3 as a starting place to assess the security of your key suppliers. Of course there are other aspects to the security and reliability of a supplier but it is wise to check their ability to keep secure and critical data that they have been entrusted with.

The form has 11 sections and it is obviously up to you if you wish to use all of it or even to add additional questions, based on the nature of your business.

Clearly you may well be dealing with suppliers of different sizes and it may be that a very small supplier is very well placed to offer you a good and reliable service. However, if they are holding very valuable data that you are responsible for, you should satisfy yourself that they are able to identify a potential security breach. The form is therefore a guide only and you are free to vary and use it as you deem appropriate for your business.

Section 1 deals with the supplier from an organisational point of view. It is designed to let you know how large they are and how many IT staff they have.

Section 2 looks at the organisation and asks if they will be storing or processing your data outside of the EU. It also asks of the company complies with the Payment Card Industry Data Security Standards (PCI DSS). Even if you do not send them any payment data, the fact that they do comply with the PCI DSS requirements should give you a high degree of confidence.

Section 3 asks about their IT Security policy and asks for a copy. Many companies will consider this document to be confidential and may refuse to hand it over. However, provided that they have a policy document you can be assured to some extent and if it has been written to a recognised standard, such as BS7799, then you can take more comfort.

Section 4 is all about access control and authentication and gives an indication of the effectiveness of the standards that they are using.

Section 5 looks at the supplier use of highly privileged accounts. All computer systems need to use highly privileged accounts but it is important that they are controlled to reduce the risk of a security breach by a hacker posing as a valid member of staff.

Section 6 asks about the controls in place on the network. In particular, does the supplier control their own network or is this outsourced. Do they use zoning within their network to protect the data from a hacker.

Section 7 deals with data encryption and asks what standards the supplier is using, including wireless access.

Section 8 looks at the patching regime that the supplier uses and asks about the AV systems that they use. It also asks about white-listing and if this is used it should be in addition to AV.

Section 9 looks at the auditing and monitoring that is in place. Question 9 looks at the way that audit logs are kept and secured. These would be vital if there were to be a security breach as the audit logs could be the starting point of an investigation.

Section 10 is looking at Internet facing web-sites and asks about how these are segregated.

Section 11 looks at the physical security and asks about the backup facilities.

Many of the questions that are asked will be quite technical and it may be that you do not have the knowledge to fully assess the answers but we have provided a scoring guide that should allow you to assess if your data is at risk and to gain some assurance from their answers. This form is not a "teach yourself IT Security" and it doesn't try to be that but if a supplier is entrusted with your data, they should be able to give you a reasonable level of assurance.

New Customer risks.

You need to assess the risk from a new customer if the customer is likely to represent a large uplift in your capacity or if you are taking on a new line. In short you need to make sure that your new customer doesn't put your company in a vulnerable position. Thinking about small suppliers who provide goods or services to a much larger company, they can get squeezed and not have an alternative other than continue to supply the large customer.

Environmental risks.

Flood prevention down-stream may increase your risk of flooding for you; this may be a real problem if your business is located in a small industrial unit for example, such as can happen when a farm uses a redundant barn for small-business use. You may find you are in an isolated area and that has a larger town down-stream and this has been protected at your expense. When there is an excess of water, it has to go somewhere and one person's flood-protection may well be another person's flood. These things are conducted on a risk-assessed basis so as to provide the best protection for the most people or for the most valuable property.

New Neighbour.

If a new company moves in next to you and is a high-risk company, you will need to see if you need to take additional steps to protect your business. There may be little you can do but be aware that there are things such as anti-social behaviour that may have an impact on you, your staff or your customers and if you can see something like that beginning to happen, you may be able to take some preventative action.

Part 6 – *What to do*

Introduction.

We have looked at a large number of possible risks that your company faces and you have put the ones you consider to relate to you into priority order. The next question is "So what can we do about them?" Only you can know how important these risks are and what impact they could have on you. If there is a risk that will have a large impact on your company and you judge that it is quite likely to occur, then you need to address it. However, needing to address a risk is not the same as needing to spend a great deal of money on it. You may be able to work in collaboration with another company to gain mutual protection. You may, for example, wish to locate a fire-resistant safe in a location away from your company but closer than your home. Is there a similar sized company that you can work with to hold their safe while they hold yours so you both achieve a good level of protection?

If you have a particular piece of machinery that you are dependent on and it could be damaged in the event of an incident, such as a flood. You could speak to your equipment supplier and see if there is another near-by company with the same equipment that you could have a mutual backup agreement with so that you provide each other with a backup facility in the event of a disaster happening. As well as protecting your business you also need to protect your budget. There will be some things that you will need to pay for but it is worth while looking at low-cost or free options first.

We will look at the main types of disasters that you may face. By now you should have listed your main risks so this should be a check-list that you have already covered.

So What?

It is important to keep things in proportion. If you are likely to suffer a power outage of a few hours but very unlikely to have more than this you may well say "So what?" If, on the other hand, you are working in a geographically remote location where your power is delivered via overhead power lines and you may suffer an outage of several days in a severe winter, then you may need to address this risk.

Only you can know your business and so only you can answer the "so what" question. This book is designed to help you prevent a disaster but you have to do this with your budgets and the financial well-being of your company in mind. Looking at the various risks you face, you should consider how long you can manage without the various facilities and services therefore judge which of the risks you need to actively avoid. Some risks you can counter by being aware of what's happening and trying to work around events.

Natural disasters:

These are things like:
    Flood – Either tidal or as a result of storm water or where a secondary problem has meant   that the flood has occurred.
    Fire – Either in your own property or in a nearby property could cause you damage. You may suffer the effects of a near-by fire such as a scrub-land blaze that is causing you disruption.
    Land-Slide – A landslide can have a direct impact on

you if your business is located part-way up a hill. It can also impact you if a land-slide causes travel disruption for you or your employees.

Weather – High winds may damage your property by bringing trees down in the vicinity of   your property or on a commuter route for you or your staff.

Snow or serious ice could well be a source of problems for you, your staff, or your   suppliers and your customers.

The way you tackle a natural disaster will depend on the type of business that you run, whether you need to deal with your customers face to face or over the Internet and whether you need to use specialist equipment to do so. If you operate an Internet based company, then you may be able to use a different location in the event of a natural disaster. The key here will be your access to a clean copy of your systems and data.

The key to disaster avoidance is knowing what things you can work without for a time and what you must have a backup for.

Pandemic.

There are several risks from a pandemic.
1)   You or your staff may become ill and leave you so short of manpower that your company can't function.
2)   You or your staff may be unable to commute to work because of restrictions having been placed on free movement of people.
3)   Your suppliers may be unable to supply you with goods or services.

4)   Your customers may be unable to come to you or may be too ill to buy your goods or services.

The result may be that you will be unable to trade normally. In the case of option 3 and 4 there is little you can do but in the case of the first 2, you may need to implement a flexible working policy. If this is the case, the pandemic plan will also deal with other potential disaster situations. By using the term "flexible working" we don't just mean working from home, though this may be the case. It means that you may need your staff to be present on-site but you may be able to change the hours of work to avoid people travelling during peak times. You may be able to allow your staff to commute outside of normal hours so they can drive, whereas normally that would not be practical. The term "flexible working" means re-thinking how your staff travel to work and seeing if they can change their work patterns OR their work location. If you allow your staff to "work from home", then take care when choosing how they can do this to make sure you're not changing one risk for another.

Legal risks.

Legal risks are things like a change of regulatory regime. If you work in a highly regulated area such as Financial Services, or the Chemical Industry, you need to keep a close eye on the nature of the regulation that you face. In most industries there are many specialist publication (often on-line) or blogs from recognised experts in the field, so provided you try to keep up to date, you shouldn't be caught out by a sudden change in regulations. However, if you don't keep up to date, then this can be a very real risk.

Technology:

We will look at IT in a separate section but the sort of technology risk that you should consider countering are things like:

Phone failure. Can you make use of mobile phones as a stop-gap measure and if so, how can you tell your customers? Can you quickly update your Web-Site to inform them?

Power failure – If you are in a vulnerable location and are likely to lose your power for an extended period, then you should be looking at a backup generator to provide you with enough power to keep your vital equipment going. If you are located in a small industrial unit, you may be able to work with your neighbours to provide a reasonable backup generator so a number of you can keep their vital services going. If you do go down this path be sure to test the generator from time to time and make sure you know who has the responsibility to keep a good supply of fuel available for the generator.

Specialist hardware failure. If you rely on specialist hardware to run your business make sure you understand your supplier's ability to provide you with replacement equipment in the event of your main units becoming unavailable. You must have a good contract in the event of you relying on a supplier to provide backup and do not expect this to be a free service.

IT Failure.

With companies becoming increasingly dependent on the Internet to promote their company and the power of a well designed web-site to make them look bigger than they are, there are a number of IT risks that would not normally be faced by a small company "In the real world". In cyber-space even a small start-up may look like a large well-established company. It may therefore look like a good place for criminals to go to steal customer records. You or your IT provider will have to understand the risks that you face and how best to counter them. There is more information in the IT risk assessment section which is in Part 2. Your network design should take into account the most likely forms of attack that you will face. If you are dealing with very sensitive intellectual property you should design your network so that the most sensitive intellectual property is not on a network that has any Internet connectivity. There has been much written about the monitoring activities of the NSA and GCHQ but you should assume that the Internet is regularly swept by most major Nation States. If you are developing a new drug that will cure Alzheimer's disease, you should not let the details of your research anywhere near an Internet connected network unless you are ready for at least one other country to "invent" the same drug just before you get yours to market. If you are developing a new games app, then you simply need to keep it secure from criminals, most nation states will not bother to exploit that sort of intellectual property.

Start with the outside and work inwards. The first thing to look at is your network design. Does this make it hard for a criminal to get to your systems and data?

Firewall.

You should use a Firewall on the outward facing portion of your network to make it harder for a criminal to gain access to your systems and data. Your Firewall needs to be correctly configured to only allow the correct ports to be open and block access to the ports that you don't use. Networks will have around 65,000 possible ports that can be used and many small companies will need under a hundred of these to be open. Some can operate with as few as ten open ports, so look at what ports are open and close as many as possible. If you are using the services of an Internet Service Provider, then ask them to check the configuration of your Firewall.

Services.

As with the open ports, there are vast numbers of services that will be installed as default in most operating systems, particularly Microsoft. Given the wide variety of computer installations that they are designing their operating systems to cater for, there are many facilities that you will not need. When there is a security flaw found in a given service, then Microsoft will correct the error and issue a patch for you to install. Even if you have a small network that you can safely install all of the Microsoft patches on, the security flaw that you are closing will be several weeks or even months old by the time you close it. Criminals will be trying to exploit the flaws as soon as they are aware of them. By closing any unused ports and removing the services that you are not using, you will be shutting a large number of potential entry points that criminals may use.

DMZ.

With most companies that trade on the Internet they will use a network with a built-in De-Militarised Zone or DMZ. To achieve this you place one Firewall at the outward facing point on your network and another behind it that will face into your network. This will give you a quarantine zone to protect your internal systems from intruders and malware. More complex networks will use a second pair of Firewalls to create zones of trust, so they may have a "red" zone that contains all the public facing web-sites and services, then an "amber" zone that contains the systems and data that is needed to keep the web-applications running and finally a "green" zone that contain all the internal systems that are used to support the business. The complexity of your network design will depend on the value of the network to your company and the risk that the contents face. Only you will know these factors but you should review your network with your IT staff or your IT supplier, or get some advice from an organisation that is there to help. Please see "Help" in a later section.

Hacking.

There is much press coverage on the activities of various hackers and hacker groups. The reality of hacking is that most hackers are professional criminals who are out to steal data in one form or another. The more complete a customer record, the more it is worth, so a customer record that simply has a name and address will not be worth much as this information can be gained from the electoral Role. If the customer records hold the name, address, data of birth, mother's maiden name and some banking data, then they will have hit the jackpot and these records will be worth a great deal to the criminal. The main aim of a hacker will be to get through the network defences and into the back-end systems, copy the data and then get out again without being detected and without using much effort. If your company has fallen victim to a professional hack, then the investigation will need to look at how they gained access and look for a "backdoor" that they will probably have installed. Often this will be a new user account that they can use to return. In some cases this will be to open a port in your Firewalls they can use to get back into your systems.

The process of closing any unused Firewall ports and removing any unused services is known as "**hardening**". All commercial networks and computers should be hardened as a cost effective way of making them less attractive to criminals. The process of installing the latest security updates from the application manufacturers is known as "**patching**". So the mantra of all IT Security professionals is "**harden and patch**" because this is a very cost-effective way of making the job of the hacker harder.

As most serious IT security failures will result in your data being copied by criminals or in some cases, by Nation States, we will look at what you can do to reduce the risk of your data being stolen and then look at what you can do to discover that it has been taken as early as possible.

Firstly we will look at the types of steps you can take to protect your data (and your IT systems). In Part 2 we looked at the various types of Malware (virus, Trojan etc.) and how they are able to infect networks. After this we will look at the ways of identifying if your data is under attack or has been taken.

Broadband failure.

If you are in an area that is prone to outages, can you make use of an external 3G or 4G dongle so you still have a basic Broadband capability?

Malware.

Never, but absolutely never open an attachment in an e-mail or click on an embedded link unless you are sure that it is friendly. It is a simple task to forge the headers of an e-mail, so getting an e-mail that seems to be from a friend or a trusted business contact doesn't mean that they sent it. Always check first, even if that means calling or texting them to check that they really did send the e-mail. If they didn't, then they need to check to see if their e-mail account has been taken over. In the case of web-browsing, try not to use a powerful account when you are looking at the Internet. With many windows systems, the main user account will be a privileged account, so that it will have the authority to install and run software and make changes to the system settings. For most uses this is too much power to have as a default, it is safer to have your main account running with very little authority, so that it would be unable to install any malware. If you need to install new software, then you should switch user accounts to a highly privileged account for that task and then switch back to your default account. If you have high-value data (personal or intellectual) you should consider using additional protection.

Anti-Virus (AV).

AV systems operate on a black-list approach. They have a list of "known-bad" code patterns that they will block. This is fine in principle but when a new piece of malware is released, the AV companies have to get hold of the code, look at it to see how it is working and install the necessary identification into their data-base of Malware and then distribute this to their clients. Even with a well funded AV company, there can be a delay of a few days while they release the updates signatures to their clients, and then the client may not have their systems set to automatically update the AV system. Even with the limitations with Av systems, you should still use a good AV system to prevent most malware from getting into your systems in the first place. Another problem that AV companies face is the growing number of virus definitions or patterns that they need to maintain. Depending on the way that the virus patterns are stored there can be hundreds of thousands of virus patterns that need to be maintained. These also need to be checked before a new piece of software can be considered "good". However, even with the problems faced by the AV industry, very few companies would consider running their IT systems without AV protection, even if they used a secondary check.

Given the limitations of AV systems that we have looked at it is worth seeing if you need additional protection. Only you will know the value of your data, but if you are holding valuable data then you should consider looking at some form of white-listing or HDF solution.

White-Listing.

White-listing systems work in the opposite way to AV in that AV looks for what is to be blocked and a white-listed solution will look at what to allow. These systems maintain a list of "known-good" applications and ONLY these will be allowed to run. If some malware gets through your defences and installs itself on your systems, then a white-listing solution should prevent it from running and alert you to the fact that it was trying to run.

Some white-listing systems work by maintaining a list of

"known good" file names and locations but criminals have been able to identify these systems and place their malicious code into the correct file and with the correct name to fool these systems. Other white-listing systems work by hashing the good code and keeping a list of locations and hash values and these are far harder to fool but they tend to have a higher overhead for the administrator to maintain the list of hash values. However, generally, white-listing has the potential to beat more malware than the traditional AV and most systems that use white-listing will also use AV as a safety-net.

Hard-Disk Firewall (HDF).

A variation on the white-list approach is the HDF that has been developed by Abatis (UK) Limited. As the criminals invest more time and effort to defeat the protection systems that companies use Abatis looked at the problems with both AV and white-listing and came up with a slightly different approach that aims to prevent new malware from getting onto the hard-drive in the first place, hence the name.

One fundamental problem with any white-listing system is the fact that it needs to load as part of the operating system start-up process. Most white-listing kernels open as "late-loading" modules because they need all of the operating system components to be running before they can start. This gives a clever criminal the option of getting their malware to open as an "early-loading" module and thus start to run before the white-listing module is operational. Almost all white-listing systems will accept any code that it finds running as trusted and so there is a way for malware to run in trusted mode. As part of the research into AV and white-listing solutions, Abatis looked at this problem and designed their HDF product to be an early-loading.

For companies holding sensitive data that criminals could be interested in, it would be worth looking at both white-listing solutions and HDF as additional protection as well as AV.

Penetration Testing.

In the section looking at your IT systems earlier in this book we looked at the various types of penetrating testing companies and how they operate. If you are trading on the Internet, or use credit or debit cards or hold valuable data, you should consider using a penetration testing company to help you assess your security and any weakness that they can find.

Active Data Protection.

One major problem that companies face is knowing if a criminal has taken a copy of their data. This is not a new problem and companies that have dealt in valuable data have always had to protect it. Way back in the middle of last century companies would sell mail-order lists. These lists of potential customers were very valuable and had to be protected. One solution was to insert false data into the lists so that they could detect if there had been any unauthorised selling of their data. With the ease of collecting on-line data today, many of these companies have disappeared but the need to protect data hasn't gone away and there are times when an old method can be extremely effective.

Let's take an example of a company that passes data to suppliers for them to use on their behalf. It is vital for the company to know that the data they send to a supplier is safe and to know if the security at the supplier has been compromised. The solution is to create a number of false customer records and these could use an existing address (your directors, family members or even company addresses) with bogus names, valid e-mail addresses that have been created for the occasion and even mobile phone numbers. So long as a register is maintained (obviously, not on the main system) with these addresses and you have a list of which addresses have been inserted into which supplier data-sets you will be in a position to see if your data have been compromised.

This works by you having some false records in your main customer data-base but when you send data to a supplier you remove your false data and insert some records that only they will have. If a copy of the customer data-base is taken by a criminal, then any contact that is attempted with one of the false customers would confirm that the data has been stolen and also tell you where it was taken from.

It is vital that the record of which addresses are sent to which supplier must be kept safe and preferably not on your main network, you don't want a criminal to steal this information.

Please remember that many data breaches are initially identified by a customer complaining that their data has been compromised. As we have worked in the financial service industry, where customer data integrity is important, the ability to know that a compromise has occurred before any customer complaints have been received is very important. With many data breaches, the way that the company treats the customers can be the difference between the company being seen as caring and professional as against one that seems to be in denial and not bothered about their customers. Survival of the company can be at stake in such cases.

Data Loss Prevention (DLP).

DLP systems are designed to prevent your data being copied without authorisation and to stop a data loss before too much harm has been done. These systems have a number of components. They will have a list of who can access what type of data, what devices are allowed to be connected to your systems and who can read, modify and delete data. They are designed to identify any unusual data movements. There are some exceptions and these are mainly in the areas of automated data movements that are sent to a wrong location or where the data is intercepted in transit. However, for most company use the ability to prevent data being copied to an unauthorised device or to identify an unusual volume of data is very valuable. In addition, the ability to know which files have been compromised (even after the event) can be very valuable.

If a hacker has gained access to your systems and starts to use a valid account to copy data, the fact that you can be warned that it is happening can mean that you can limit the loss and quickly start an investigation.

Data Backups.

For a number of reasons it is vital that your data is backed up to protect it from corruption and accidental destruction. You should plan your backup process so that you can recover your data, operating system software and application programs. How often you take your backups and where you store them should be considered carefully. You are aiming to protect your company from potential accidents, malicious actions and natural disasters so that you can continue to operate and so recover from an incident quickly.

Testing.

Make sure you regularly test that you can restore your operating system, specialist applications and your data from the backups that you have been taking. Any problems with the backup routines need to be found before you are trying to recover your systems in anger.

Staff Issues.

Many small companies suffer from a lack of staff numbers. They don't have complete departments dealing with a particular problem; they are more likely to have a single member of staff doing 2 or 3 different jobs. While this can make the individuals highly valuable and highly skilled it can also give a problem in the event of sickness, accident or a resignation. It is all too easy to leave a skilled and efficient member of staff alone, particularly when you are all busy keeping the company running. However, it is worth while looking at your key staff to see if you can cross-train them so that they are able to cover each other in the event of an accident or a natural disaster that causes some of your staff to be off work, or when the time comes for them to move on.

Documentation.

It is worth while spending some time documenting your key processes. This will achieve two things. Firstly, it will allow the owner of the process to review how they do it. There will be times when the act of documenting a process will highlight something that can be improved. The other output from documenting a process is the ability to use this as a training manual. If you have a sudden surge in demand for a process, then the ability to help your overworked member of staff by getting a co-worker to work from the manual may be the difference between fulfilling an order and not.

Suppliers.

Only you know your business and how it runs. Only you can know how reliable your suppliers are but it is worth taking some time to assess their ability to complement your company and to keep you supplied. If you are able to use 2 suppliers for a given product or process, then you will have given yourself backup in the event of a supplier failure as well as helping you deal with a sudden surge in demand for your products or services. We have provided a Supplier Review Form that is mainly designed to help you look at their security. Please feel free to modify this form for your own use so you can look at other aspects of your supplier's activities.

Conclusion.

Looking at the above suggestions, please remember that they are just examples of things that you can do to protect your systems, data and your company. There are two things that any small business need to protect, these are their reputation and their budgets. Look at the various risk areas and see what you can do to reduce or remove these without automatically reaching for the cheque-book. Secondly, look at protecting your reputation so you can identify problems early and head them off whenever you can.

Part 7 – Help

Having given you a number of problems to think about, it is worth saying that you are not without help. There are many organisations and companies that you can go for help and advice. Below is a list of some companies and organisations that we have had experience of working with. We do not recommend any particular service because in order to do so we would need to understand exactly what you are trying to achieve and the precise nature of your business. However, this should be a good starting place for you to build your knowledge. This is not meant to be an exhaustive list but simply some examples of resources that we have used over the years. Of course, if you have a particular question, then using your favourite search engine should provide you with information.

Many of the organisations we have listed will be happy to talk to small companies and give them guidance.

Cyber Security.

List of scanners and penetration testers.

Automated Scanning.

Penetration testing is simulating an attack from a hacker. Some testing companies will offer you the use of automated scanners, and these are the basic form of attack. A scanner will highlight a weakness in your security but will not automatically try to exploit it. Companies like those below offer a scanning service that is low cost and designed to be used by IT staff who can understand the brief explanations given in the reports.

Qualys – Is an automated scanner that will check your network for vulnerabilities. While this is not as thorough as a full penetration test conducted by a skilled consultant, it is thorough and generally represents good value for money. Their systems can operate to the PCI DSS standards.
www.qualys.com
Qualys also provide some useful free tools that are worth familiarising yourself with;
www.ssllabs.com will assess and score the strength of the HTTPS configuration of your website,
browsercheck.qualys.com will assess and score the security of your web browser, recommending updates for any common plug-ins.
www.qualys.com/forms/assetview is a free asset inventory tool to help you keep track of your hardware and software, which can quickly become a burden as your company grows.

Outpost24 – Is another automated scanning service provider that can assess your web presence, your internal networks, and fulfil PCI scanning requirements.
www.outpost24.com

Penetration testing.

Other penetration testers will conduct more sophisticated attacks and will use a variety of tools that the hackers will deploy. They may use a scanner but will go on to use a mix of **social engineering** tricks to try to fool your staff into giving out information and then exploit this. While this may seem a bit underhand, please remember that if a consultant can trick your staff into giving out information, then a skilled hacker will also succeed. The advantage of using a consultant to do it is the fact that they will then explain how they got the information and how an attacker would use it. These attacks can become very valuable lessons to train your staff. The thing to remember with social engineering is that it is normally conducted over the phone. If the staff member becomes suspicious, the attacker can simply hang-up and try another person later. The motto seems to be "Before you find your handsome Prince you have to kiss a lot of Frogs!"

ProCheckUp – ProCheckUp has a wealth of experience in Cyber Security consulting and specialise in manual and automated penetration testing. They have developed their own specialised knowledge based scanner that they use before confirming the results with manual checks. They operate to very high IT industry standards such as CREST, CESG, CHECK and PCI DSS. For more information see www.procheckup.com

NCC and **ContextIS** are both long established organisation with international reach and a diverse range of services in the information security world, each with membership of several select committees and response groups ensuring that they are able to accommodate any eventuality. Visit www.nccgroup.trust and www.contextis.com for further information.

Information Risk Management – IRM was founded in 1998 and have therefore been around for a long time in the Cyber Security world. They have offices in London and Cheltenham so that they can be close to their main customers. They offer some innovative solutions and operate to CREST, CESG, CHECK and PCI DSS standards. For more information visit www.irmplc.com

Physically penetrating your buildings.

The next level of attack comes from the companies who will try to gain physical access to your building. For most small companies this is a hard task because the staff working for you will tend to know all of the other employees. However, for a larger company, the ability to keep the bad guys out can be vital. Some of the most successful hacks in history started with a member of staff telling the attacker their user name and password. If an attacker can gain access to your building, they will be inside your IT network and can generally attach a device directly into your trusted (green) network zone. This is not an issue for most small companies but if you are holding very high value data, then you need to be aware of the tricks that the enemy will use.

First-Base – First Base is a well established company that uses a mixture of social engineering, physical penetration tests to try to gain access to your systems. They will also use "conventional" hacking tools. They are based in West Sussex on the south coast of England, but like all companies that operate in Cyber Space, can work anywhere the client requires. For more information visit www.firstbase.co.uk

Investigations

So what do you do if you believe your systems have been attacked, or even hacked? The following are companies you can call if you believe you have a problem or are at risk. They employ experienced investigators and can offer advice in confidence.

ESID Consulting – Is an independent specialist in all aspects of Internal / Workplace and Anti-Corruption Investigations, Information Security and Business Continuity.

The company has specialist knowledge in carrying out employee investigations and digital forensics, where theft, misuse and "leakage" of corporate data and other sensitive information has occurred. They provide practical support and advice on securing your company data and protecting your business and clients' information.

They achieve this through the creation and implementation of an appropriate Business Continuity Plan and Information Security Management System, or a review of your current arrangements www.esid.co.uk

Physical intrusion, investigations and corporate protection

XIX Group – This is a specialist company that offers risk management solutions to corporate organisations and individuals. They are able to test your physical security, your disaster planning and train your staff in a variety of security related skills. If you have suffered a security breach, they can investigate and often help you to minimise the impact of the loss. Employing a number of Ex-Metropolitan Police specialists, they can often help companies regain control in what can be a fast moving incident. www.xixgroup.com

They will identify risks to high-profile people and conduct counter surveillance on high-risk companies and individuals.

Your company reputation.

We looked at what your customers and employees think about your company and what they publish about you earlier in the book. It is wise to use a search engine to look for your company name as well as looking on any trade web-sites where reviews are published. If you use market-place companies like E-Bay or Amazon, then monitor your reputation and you should review sites like www.glassdoor.co.uk to see what your employees and ex-employees are saying.

Publications

There are a number of publications that you can access over the Internet that will help you understand the various security threats and see what the latest attacks are.

The Register – is an online publication that looks at a number of IT topics, including security. To obtain a daily copy you will need to register but the publication is free. Go to www.theregister.co.uk for the main web-site or to account.theregister.co.uk to sign-up for your choice of topics.

SC Magazine – has a number of articles and reviews of Cyber Security products and well as explaining some of the key issues. www.scmagazineuk.com

Infosecurity Magazine – is another online magazine that offers news and comment to Cyber Security professionals. It is a good source of information. For more information go to www.infosecurity-magazine.com

As with online publications, there are a number of organisations that will help with your Cyber Security needs.

US-CERT – is an American organisation and the initials stand for United States Computer Emergency Readiness Team. They offer a number of white-papers and articles about various aspects of Cyber Security and most of their publications are free. You can also subscribe to their alerting system by giving your e-mail address.

AV Systems
Before investing in an anti-virus platform to help protect your systems and data you may want to review performance, keeping in mind that no AV tool will provide 100% protection and that the effectiveness of any tool varies up or down over time. Two independent websites which conduct regular tests of AV effectiveness are www.av-test.org and www.av-comparatives.org

Microsoft Security Essentials comes as standard with any modern version of Windows
Symantec – www.symantec.com
Kaspersky – www.kaspersky.com
McCafee – www.mccafee.com

White-Lists
Lumension Application and device control – www.lumension.com

HDF
Abatis – www.abatis-HDF.com

Vendors
Rather than setting up relationships with many various IT

organisations for products and support it may be beneficial to get in touch with a vendor who can provide a one-stop-shop type of approach. Vendors are typically independent and have relationships with a variety of service providers so that they can tailor a solution to suit your specific needs, they often also have some consulting capabilities to help you get set up and some first line support capabilities for when things go wrong. While there are many vendors on the market you might want to take a look at ww.foursys.co.uk and www.nonstopit.com to get started.

The Police

There are a number of specialist police units at a regional and a national level that you can turn to if you believe you have suffered a security breach. The National Cyber Crime Unit will investigate serious cyber attacks and each police region has their own regional organised crime unit who will respond to a report of serious cyber criminal activity.

Regulators and supporting organisations

PCI – Payment Card Industry www.pcisecuritystandards.org
ICO – The Information Commissioner's Office
www.ico.org.uk
SANS Institute www.sans.org
OWASP – Open Web Application Security Project
www.owasp.org
Your MP and MEP (or **MSP** in Scotland)

Organisations that will help small businesses

Cyber Security Clusters – There are a number of Cyber Security Clusters around the UK and these are aimed at helping small businesses working in the Cyber Security sector. However, the various members of your local cluster may well provide a good source of help and advice on your IT Security issues. www.ukcybersecurityforum.com

The Federation of Small Businesses – Is an organisation that is designed to help small businesses. They can give advice and guidance to small businesses on a variety of matters. www.fsb.org.uk

British Computer Society – Is the Chartered Institute for IT. It has a number of local branches and specialist sections and is a good starting point for increasing your IT skills. The branch meetings and presentations are generally open to members and non-members alike, so it can be a good source of information and assistance. www.bcs.org.uk

Government – The government has a **Minister for small business, industry and enterprise.** https://www.gov.uk/government/ministers/minister-of-state-business-and-enterprise

Have I Been Pwned – Is a free subscription/notification website that will alert you if your email address (or any email address on your business domain) is exposed in a public data breach such as that which affected Adobe or Ashley Madison. Getting ahead of the curve can help you to take preventative or recovery measures before any damage is done, such as resetting passwords for the exposed accounts. www.haveibeenpwned.com *(The term Pwned came about because of a typing error in a games review where the author meant to type "owned" and wrote "pwned" instead, the term stuck)*

124

There are also a number of Government publications aimed at assisting small businesses with their Cyber security. Please see Appendix A for the "Government 10 steps to cyber security".

Check your favourite Internet search engine for the latest advice.

Conclusion

The form that was used in Part 3 and is available from www.disaster-avoidance.co.uk for you to download and modify for your own use.

Appendix A

Advice from HMG

The following document is from www.CPNI.Gov.UK and contains advice to companies about how to secure their Cyber resources. While the document is designed to work for all companies some of the advice will be more applicable to larger organisations. However, there is much that is worth reading and it will provide helpful advice as your company grows. It is always worth checking for the latest advice from the government by looking at www.CPNI.Gov.UK regularly.

10 Steps To Cyber Security: Information Risk Management Regime

Detailed cyber security information and advice concerning your organisation's information risk management regime.

Summary

It is best practice for an organisation to apply the same degree of rigour to assessing the risks to its information assets as it would to legal, regulatory, financial or operational risk. This can be achieved by embedding an information risk management regime across the organisation, which is actively supported by the Board, senior managers and an empowered Information Assurance (IA) governance structure. Defining and communicating the organisation's attitude and approach to risk management
is crucial. Boards may wish to consider communicating their

risk appetite statement and information risk management policy across the organisation to ensure that employees, contractors and suppliers are aware of the organisation's risk management boundaries.

What is the risk?

Risk is an inherent part of doing business. For any organisation to operate successfully it needs to address risk and respond proportionately and appropriately to a level which is consistent with the organisation's risk appetite. If an organisation does not identify and manage risk it can lead to business failure. A lack of effective information risk management and governance may lead to the following:

Increased exposure to risk

Information risk must be owned at Board level. Without effective risk governance processes it is impossible for the Board to understand the risk exposure of the organisation. The Board must be confident that information risks are being managed within tolerance throughout the lifecycle of deployed systems or services

Missed business opportunities

Where risk decisions are being taken at junior level without effective governance and ownership back to senior levels, it may promote an overly cautious approach to information risk which may lead to missed business opportunities. Alternatively, an overly open approach may expose the organisation to unacceptable risks

Ineffective policy implementation

An organisation's Board has overall ownership of the corporate security policy. Without effective risk management and governance processes the Board will not have confidence that its stated policy is being consistently applied across the business as a whole

Poor reuse of security investment

A lack of effective governance means that information risk management activities may be undertaken locally when they could be more effectively deployed at an organisational level

How can the risk be managed?

Establish a governance framework

A governance framework needs to be established that enables and supports a consistent and empowered approach to information risk management across the organisation, with ultimate responsibility for risk ownership residing at Board level.

Determine the organisation's risk appetite

Agree the level of information risk the organisation is prepared to tolerate in pursuit of its business objectives and produce a risk appetite statement to help guide information risk management decisions throughout the business.

Maintain the Board's engagement with information risk

The risks to the organisation's information assets from a cyber attack should be a regular agenda item for Board discussion. To ensure senior ownership and oversight, the risk of cyber attack should be documented in the corporate risk register and regularly reviewed; entering into knowledge sharing partnerships with other companies and law enforcement can help you in understanding new and emerging threats that might be a risk to your own business and also to share mitigations that might work.

Produce supporting policies

An overarching corporate information risk policy needs to be created and owned by the Board to help communicate and support risk management objectives, setting out the information risk management strategy for the organisation as a whole.

Adopt a lifecycle approach to information risk management

The components of a risk can change over time so a continuous through-life process needs to be adopted to ensure security controls remain appropriate to the risk.

Apply recognised standards

Consider the application of recognised sources of security management good practice, such as the ISO/IEC 27000 series of standards, and implement physical, personnel, procedural and technical measures.

Make use of endorsed assurance schemes

Consider adopting the Cyber Essentials Scheme. It provides

guidance on the basic controls that should be put in place and offers a certification process that demonstrates your commitment to cyber risk management.

Educate users and maintain their awareness

All users have a responsibility to manage the risks to the organisation's Information and Communications Technologies (ICT) and information assets. Provide appropriate training and user education that is relevant to their role and refresh it regularly; encourage staff to participate in knowledge sharing exchanges with peers across business and Government.

Promote a risk management culture

Risk management needs to be organisation-wide, driven by corporate governance from the top down, with user participation demonstrated at every level of the business.

10 Steps To Cyber Security: Secure Configuration

Detailed cyber security information and advice concerning the secure configuration of your organisation.

Summary

By putting in place corporate policies and processes to develop secure baseline builds and manage the configuration and the ongoing functionality of all Information and Communications Technologies (ICT), organisations can greatly improve the security of their ICT systems. Good corporate practice is to develop a strategy to remove or disable unnecessary functionality from ICT systems and keep them patched against known vulnerabilities. Failure to do so is likely to result in increased exposure of the business and its ICT to threats and vulnerabilities and therefore increased risk to the confidentiality, integrity and availability of systems and information.

What is the risk?

Establishing and then actively maintaining the secure configuration of ICT systems should be seen as a key security control. ICT systems that are not locked down, hardened or patched will be particularly vulnerable to attacks that may be easily prevented.

Organisations that fail to produce and implement corporate security policies that manage the secure configuration and patching of their ICT systems are subject to the following risks:

Unauthorised changes to systems

An attacker could make unauthorised changes to ICT systems or information, compromising confidentiality, availability and integrity

Exploitation of unpatched vulnerabilities

New patches are released almost daily and the timely application of security patches is critical to preserving the confidentiality, integrity and availability of ICT systems. Attackers will attempt to exploit unpatched systems to provide them with unauthorised access to system resources and information. Many successful attacks are enabled by exploiting a vulnerability for which a patch had been issued prior to the attack taking place

Exploitation of insecure system configurations

An attacker could exploit a system that has not been locked down or hardened by:

1. Gaining unauthorised access to information assets or importing malware
2. Exploiting unnecessary functionality that has not been removed or disabled to conduct
3. attacks and gain unauthorised access to systems, services, resources and information
4. Connecting unauthorised equipment to exfiltrate information or introduce malware
5. Creating a back door to use in the future for malicious purposes

Increases in the number of security incidents

Without an awareness of vulnerabilities that have been identified and the availability (or not) of patches and fixes, the business will be increasingly disrupted by security incidents

How can the risk be managed?

Develop corporate policies to update and patch systems
Use the latest versions of operating systems, web browsers and applications. Develop and implement corporate policies to ensure that security patches are applied in a timeframe that is commensurate with the organisation's overall risk management approach. Organisations should use automated patch management and software update tools.

Create and maintain hardware and software inventories

Create inventories of the authorised hardware and software that constitute ICT systems across the organisation. Ideally, suitably configured automated tools should be used to capture the physical location, the business owner and the purpose of the hardware together with the version and patching status of all software used on the system. The tools should also be used to identify any unauthorised hardware or software, which should be removed.

Lock down operating systems and software

Consider the balance between system usability and security and then document and implement a secure baseline build for all ICT systems, covering clients, mobile devices, servers, operating systems, applications and network devices such as firewalls and routers. Essentially, any services, functionality or applications that are not required to support the business should be removed or disabled. The secure build profile should be managed by the configuration control and management process and any deviation from the standard build should be documented and formally approved.

Conduct regular vulnerability scans

Organisations should run automated vulnerability scanning tools against all networked devices regularly and remedy any identified vulnerabilities within an agreed time frame. Organisations should also maintain their situational awareness of the threats and vulnerabilities they face.

Establish configuration control and management

Produce policies and procedures that define and support the configuration control and change management requirements for all ICT systems, including software.

Disable unnecessary input/output devices and removable media access

Assess business requirements for user access to input/output devices and removable media (this could include MP3 players and Smart phones). Disable ports and system functionality that is not needed by the business (which may include USB ports, CD/DVD/Card media drives)

Implement whitelisting and execution control

Create and maintain a whitelist of authorised applications and software that can be executed on ICT systems. In addition, ICT systems need to be capable of preventing the installation and execution of unauthorised software and applications by employing process execution controls, software application arbiters and only accepting code that is signed by trusted suppliers;

Limit user ability to change configuration

Provide users with the minimum system rights and permissions that they need to fulfil their business role. Users with 'normal' privileges should be prevented from installing or disabling any software or services running on the system.

10 Steps To Cyber Security: Network Security

Detailed cyber security information and advice concerning your organisation's network security.

Summary

Connecting to untrusted networks (such as the Internet) exposes corporate networks to attacks that seek to compromise the confidentiality, integrity and availability of Information and Communications Technologies (ICT) and the information they store and process. This can be prevented by developing policies and risk management approaches to protect corporate networks by applying security controls that are commensurate with the risks that have been identified and the organisation's risk appetite.

What is the risk?

Corporate networks need to be protected against both internal and external threats. The level to which networks are protected should be considered in the context of the organisation's risk appetite, risk assessment and corporate security policies. Businesses that fail to protect their networks appropriately could be subject to a number of risks, including:

Leakage of sensitive corporate information

Poor network design could be exploited by both internal and external attackers to compromise information or conduct unauthorised releases of sensitive information resulting in compromises in confidentiality, integrity and availability

Import and export of malware

Failure to put in place appropriate boundary security controls could lead to the import of malware and the compromise of business systems. In addition, users could deliberately or accidentally release malware or other malicious content to business partners or the general public via network connections that are poorly designed and managed

Denial of service

Networks that are connected to untrusted networks (such as the Internet) are vulnerable to denial of services attacks, where access to services and information is denied to legitimate users, compromising the availability of the system or service

Exploitation of vulnerable systems

Attackers will exploit poorly protected networks to gain unauthorised access to compromise the confidentiality, integrity and availability of systems, services and information

Damage or defacement of corporate resources

Attackers that have successfully compromised the network can damage internal and externally facing systems and information (such as defacing corporate websites), harming the organisation's reputation and customer confidence

How can the risk be managed?

Produce, implement and maintain network security policies that align with the organisation's broader information risk management policies and objectives. Follow recognised network design principles (ie ISO/IEC 27033-1:2009) to help define the necessary security qualities for the perimeter and internal network segments and ensure that all network devices are configured to the secure baseline build.

Police the network perimeter

Limit access to network ports, protocols and applications filtering and inspecting all traffic at the network perimeter to ensure that only traffic which is required to support the business is being exchanged. Control and manage all inbound and outbound network connections and deploy technical controls to scan for malware and other malicious content.

Install firewalls

Firewalls should be deployed to form a buffer zone between the untrusted external network and the internal network used by the business. The firewall rule set should deny traffic by default and a whitelist should be applied that only allows authorised protocols, ports and applications to communicate with authorised networks and network addresses. This will reduce the exposure of ICT systems to network based attacks.

Prevent malicious content

Deploy antivirus and malware checking solutions to examine both inbound and outbound data at the perimeter in addition to antivirus and malware protection deployed on internal networks and on host systems. The antivirus and malware solutions used at the perimeter should be different to those used to protect internal networks and systems in order to provide some additional defence in depth.

Protect the internal network

Ensure that there is no direct network connectivity between internal systems and systems hosted on untrusted networks (such as the Internet), limit the exposure of sensitive information and monitor network traffic to detect and react to attempted and actual network intrusions.

Segregate network as sets

Identify, group and isolate critical business information assets and services and apply appropriate network security controls to them.

Secure wireless devices

Wireless devices should only be allowed to connect to trusted wireless networks. All wireless access points should be secured. Security scanning tools should have the ability to detect and locate unauthorised wireless access points.

Protect internal Internet Protocol (IP) addresses

Implement capabilities (such as Network Address Translation) to prevent internal IP addresses from being exposed to external networks and attackers and ensure that it is not possible to route network traffic directly from untrusted networks to internal networks.

Enable secure administration

Administrator access to any network component should only be carried out over dedicated network infrastructure and secure channels using communication protocols that support encryption.

Configure the exception handling processes

Ensure that error messages returned to internal or external systems or users do not include sensitive information that may be useful to attackers.

Monitor the network

Tools such as network intrusion detection and network intrusion prevention should be placed on the network and configured by qualified staff to monitor traffic for unusual or malicious incoming and outgoing activity that could be indicative of an attack or an attempt. Alerts generated by the system should be promptly managed by appropriately trained staff.

Assurance processes

Conduct regular penetration tests of the network infrastructure and undertake simulated cyber attack exercises to ensure that all security controls have been implemented correctly and are providing the necessary levels of security.

10 Steps To Cyber Security: Managing User Privileges

Detailed cyber security information and advice concerning how to manage user privileges within you organisation.

Summary

It is good practice for an organisation to manage the access privileges that users have to an Information and Communications Technologies (ICT), the information it holds and the services it provides. All users of ICT systems should only be provided with the privileges that they need to do their job. This principle is often referred to as 'Least Privilege'. A failure to manage user privileges appropriately may result in an increase in the number of deliberate and accidental attacks.

What is the risk?

Businesses and organisations should understand what access employees need to information, services and resources in order to do their job. Otherwise they will not be able to grant ICT system rights and permissions to individual users or groups of users that are proportionate to their role within the organisation. Failure to effectively manage user privileges could result in the following risks being realised:

Misuse of privileges

Authorised users can misuse the privileges assigned to them to either deliberately or accidentally compromise ICT systems. For example to make unauthorised changes to the configuration of systems, leading to a loss of the confidentiality, integrity or availability of information or ICT systems

Increased attacker capability

Attackers will use unused or compromised user accounts to carry out their attacks and, if allowed to, they will return and reuse the compromised account on numerous occasions, or sell the access to others. The system privileges provided to the original user of the compromised account will be available to the attacker to use. Ultimately attackers will seek to gain access to root or administrative accounts to allow them full access to all system information, services and resources

Negating established security controls

Where attackers have privileged access to ICT systems they will attempt to cover their tracks by making changes to security controls or deleting accounting and audit logs so that their activities are not detected

How can the risk be managed?

Set up a personnel screening process

All users need to undergo some form of pre-employment screening to a level that is commensurate with the sensitivity of the information they will have access to.

Establish effective account management processes

Corporate processes and procedures should manage and review user accounts from creation and modification through to eventual deletion when a member of staff leaves. Unused or dormant accounts, perhaps provided for temporary staff or for testing purposes, should be removed or suspended in-line with corporate policy.

Establish policy and standards for user identification and access control

The quality of user passwords and their lifecycle should be determined by a corporate policy. Ideally they should be machine generated, randomised passwords. If this is not possible, password complexity rules should be enforced by the system. For some ICT systems an additional authentication factor (such as a physical token) may be necessary and this should be identified in the risk assessment. Access controls should be allocated on the basis of business need and 'Least Privilege'.

Limit user privileges

Users should only be provided with the rights and permissions to systems, services, information and resources that they need to fulfil their business role.

Limit the number and use of privileged accounts

Strictly control the number of privileged accounts for roles such as system or database administrators. Ensure that this type of account is not used for high risk or day to day user activities, for example to gain access to external e-mail or browse the Internet. Provide administrators with normal accounts for business use. The requirement to hold a privileged account should be reviewed more frequently than 'standard user' accounts.

Monitor all users

Monitor user activity, particularly all access to sensitive information and the use of privileged account actions, such as the creation of new user accounts, changes to user passwords or the deletion of accounts and audit logs.

Limit access to the audit system and the system activity logs

Activity logs from network devices should be sent to a dedicated accounting and audit system that is separated from the core network. Access to the audit system and the logs should be strictly controlled to preserve the integrity and availability of the content and all privileged user access recorded.

Educate users and maintain their awareness

Without exception, all users should be aware of the policy regarding acceptable account usage and their personal responsibility to adhere to corporate security policies and the disciplinary measures that could be applied for failure to do so.

10 Steps To Cyber Security: User Education and Awareness

Detailed cyber security information and advice concerning user education and awareness within your organisation.

Summary

Unfortunately the use made by employees of an organisation's Information and Communications Technologies (ICT) brings with it various risks. It is critical for all staff to be aware of their personal security responsibilities and the requirement to comply with corporate security policies. This can be achieved through systematic delivery of a security training and awareness programme that actively seeks to increase the levels of security expertise and knowledge across the organisation as well as a security-conscious culture.

What is the risk?

Organisations that do not produce user security policies or train their users in recognised good security practices will be vulnerable to many of the following risks:

Unacceptable use

Without a clear policy on what is considered to be acceptable, certain actions by users may contravene good security practice and could lead to the compromise of personal or sensitive commercial information that could result in legal or regulatory sanctions and reputational damage

Removable media and personally owned devices

Unless it is clearly set out in policy and regularly communicated, staff may consider it acceptable to use their own removable media or connect their personal devices to the corporate infrastructure. This could potentially lead to the import of malware and the compromise of personal or sensitive commercial information

Legal and regulatory sanction

If users are not aware of any special handling or the reporting requirements for particular classes of sensitive information the organisation may be subject to legal and regulatory sanctions

Incident reporting

If users do not report incidents promptly the impact of any incident could be compounded

Security Operating Procedures

If users are not trained in the secure use of their organisation's ICT systems or the functions of a security control, they may accidentally misuse the system, potentially compromising a security control and the confidentiality, integrity and availability of the information held on the system

External attack

Users remain the weakest link in the security chain and they will always be a primary focus for a range of attacks (phishing, social engineering, etc) because, when compared to a technical attack, there is a greater likelihood of success and the attacks are cheaper to mount. In many instances, a successful attack only requires one user to divulge a logon credential or open an e-mail with malicious content

Insider threat

A significant change in an employee's personal situation could make them vulnerable to coercion and they may release personal or sensitive commercial information to others. Dissatisfied users may try to abuse their system level privileges or coerce other users, to gain access to information or systems to which they are not authorised. Equally, they may attempt to steal or physically deface computer resources

How can the risk be managed?

Produce a user security policy

The organisation should develop and produce a user security policy (as part of their overarching corporate security policy) that covers acceptable use. Security procedures for all ICT systems should be produced that are appropriate and relevant to all business roles and processes.

Establish a staff induction process

New users (including contractors and third party users) should be made aware of their personal responsibility to comply with the corporate security policies as part of the induction process. The terms and conditions for their employment (contracts for contractors and third party users) must be formally acknowledged and retained to support any subsequent disciplinary action. Ideally, the initial user registration process should also be linked to the organisation's technical access controls.

Maintain user awareness of the cyber risks faced by the organisation

Without exception, all users should receive regular refresher training on the cyber risks to the organisation and to them as both employees and individuals.

Support the formal assessment of Information Assurance (IA) skills

Staff in security roles should be encouraged to develop and formally validate their IA skills through enrolment on a recognised certification scheme for IA Professionals. Some security related roles such as system administrators, incident management team members and forensic investigators will require specialist training.

Monitor the effectiveness of security training

Establish mechanisms to test the effectiveness and value of the security training provided to all staff. This should be done through formal feedback and potentially by including questions in the staff survey on security training and the organisation's security culture. Those areas that regularly feature in security reports or achieve the lowest feedback ratings should be targeted for remedial action.

Promote an incident reporting culture

The organisation should enable a security culture that

empowers staff to voice their concerns about poor security practices and security incidents to senior managers, without fear of recrimination.

Establish a formal disciplinary process

All staff should be made aware that any abuse of the organisation's security policies will result in disciplinary action being taken against them.

10 Steps To Cyber Security: Incident Management

Detailed cyber security information and advice concerning incident management within your organisation.

Summary

All organisations will experience an information security incident at some point. Investment in establishing effective incident management policies and processes will help to improve resilience, support business continuity, improve customer and stakeholder confidence and reduce any financial impact.

What is the risk?

Security incidents are inevitable and they will vary in their business impact. All incidents need to be effectively managed, particularly those that invoke the organisation's disaster recovery and business continuity plans. Some incidents can, on further analysis, be indicative of more severe underlying problems. If businesses fail to implement an incident management capability that can detect, manage and analyse security incidents the following risks could be realised:

A major disruption of business operations

Failure to realise that an incident has occurred and manage it effectively may compound the impact of the incident, leading to a long term outage, serious financial loss and erosion of customer confidence

Continual business disruption

An organisation that fails to address the root cause of incidents by addressing weaknesses in the corporate security architecture could be exposed to consistent and damaging business disruption

Failure to comply with legal and regulatory reporting requirements

An incident resulting in the compromise of sensitive information covered by mandatory reporting controls that are not adhered to could lead to legal or regulatory penalties. The organisation's business profile will determine the type and nature of incidents that may occur, and the impact they will have, and so a risk-based approach that considers all business processes should be used to shape the incident management plans. In addition, the quality and effectiveness of the security policies and the standards applied by the organisation will also be contributing factors to preventing incidents.

How can the risk be managed?

Obtain senior management approval and backing

The organisation's Board needs to understand the risks and benefits of incident management and provide appropriate funding to resource it and lead the delivery.

Establish an incident response capability

The organisation should identify the funding and resources to develop, deliver and maintain an organisation-wide incident management capability that can address the full range of incidents that could occur. This capability could be outsourced to a reputable supplier, such as those on the Cyber Incident Response (CIR) scheme. The supporting policy processes and plans should be risk based and cover any legal and regulatory reporting or data accountability requirements.

Provide specialist training

The incident response team may need specialist knowledge and expertise across a number of technical (including forensic investigation) and non-technical areas. The organisation should identify recognised sources of specialist incident management training and maintain the organisation's skill base.

Define the required roles and responsibilities

The organisation needs to appoint and empower specific individuals (or suppliers) to handle ICT incidents and provide them with clear terms of reference to manage any type of incident that may occur.

Establish a data recovery capability

Data losses occur and so a systematic approach to the backup of the corporate information asset base should be implemented. Backup media should be held in a physically secure location on-site and off-site where at all possible and the ability to recover archived data for operational use should be regularly tested.

Test the incident management plans

All plans supporting security incident management (including Disaster Recover and Business Continuity) should be regularly tested. The outcome of the tests should be used to inform the development and gauge the effectiveness of the incident management plans.

Decide what information will be shared and with whom

For information bound by specific legal and regulatory requirements the organisation may have to report any incidents that affect the status of that information within a specific timeframe. All internal and external reporting requirements should be clearly identified in the Incident Management Plans.

Collect and analyse post-incident evidence

The preservation and analysis of the user or network activity that led up to the event is critical to identify and remedy the root cause of an incident. The collected evidence could potentially support any follow on disciplinary or legal action and the incident management policy needs to set out clear guidelines to follow that comply with a recognised code of practice.

Conduct a lessons learned review

Log the actions taken during an incident and review the performance of the incident management process post incident (or following a test) to see what aspects worked well and what could be improved. Review the organisational response and update any related security policy, process or user training that could have prevented the incident from occurring.

Educate users and maintain their awareness

All users should be made aware of their responsibilities and the procedures they should follow to report and respond to an incident. Equally, all users should be encouraged to report any security weaknesses or incident as soon as possible and without fear of recrimination.

Report criminal incidents to Law Enforcement
It is important that online crimes are reported to Action Fraud or the relevant law enforcement agency to build a clearer view of the national threat picture and deliver an appropriate response.

10 Steps To Cyber Security: Malware Prevention
Detailed cyber security information and advice concerning malware prevention within your organisation.

Summary

Any information exchange carries a degree of risk as it could expose the organisation to malicious code and content (malware) which could seriously damage the confidentiality, integrity and availability of the organisation's information and Information and Communications Technologies (ICT) on which it is hosted. The risk may be reduced by implementing security controls to manage the risks to all business activities.

What is the risk?

Malware infections can result in the disruption of business services, the unauthorised export of sensitive information, material financial loss and legal or regulatory sanctions. The range, volume and originators of information exchanged with the business and the technologies that support them provide a range of opportunities for malware to be imported. Examples include:

E-mail

Still provides the primary path for internal and external information exchange. It can be used for targeted or random attacks (phishing) through malicious file attachments that will release their payload when the file is opened or contain embedded links that redirect the recipient to a website that then downloads malicious content

Web browsing and access to social media

Uncontrolled browsing, including access to social media websites and applications, could provide an opportunity for an attacker to direct malicious content to a individual user or lead to the download of malicious content from a compromised or malicious website

Removable media and personally owned devices

Malware can be transferred to a corporate ICT system through the use of removable media or the connection of a personally owned device

How can the risk be managed?

Develop and publish corporate policies

Develop and implement policies, standards and processes that deliver the overall risk management objectives but directly address the business processes that are vulnerable to malware.

Establish anti-malware defences across the organisation

Agree a top level corporate approach to managing the risk from malware that is applicable and relevant to all business areas.

Scan for malware across the organisation

Protect all host and client machines with antivirus solutions that will actively scan for malware.

Manage all data import and export

All information supplied to or from the organisation electronically should be scanned for malicious content.

Blacklist malicious websites

Ensure that the perimeter gateway uses blacklisting to block access to known malicious websites.

Provide dedicated media scanning machines

Standalone workstations (with no network connectivity) should be provided and equipped with two antivirus products. The workstation should be capable of scanning the content contained on any type of media and, ideally, every scan should be traceable to an individual.

Establish malware defences

Malware can attack any system process or function so the adoption of security architecture principles that provide multiple defensive layers (defence-in-depth) should be considered. The following controls are considered essential to manage the risks from malware:

Deploy antivirus and malicious code checking solutions with capabilities to continuously scan inbound and outbound objects at the perimeter, on internal networks and on host systems, preferably using different products at each layer. This will increase detection capabilities whilst reducing risks posed by any deficiencies in individual products. Any suspicious or infected objects should be quarantined for further analysis.

Deploy a content filtering capability on all external gateways to try to prevent attackers delivering malicious code to the common desktop applications used by the user, the web browser being a prime example. Content filtering can also help to counter the risks from a compromised information release mechanism or authorisation process that may allow sensitive data to be sent to external networks.

Install firewalls on the host and gateway devices and configure them to deny traffic by default, allowing only connectivity associated with known white listed applications

If the business processes can support it, disable scripting languages such as Windows Scripting, Active X, VBScript and JavaScript. Where possible, disable the auto run function to prevent the automatic import of malicious code from any type of removable media. Equally, if removable media is introduced, the system should automatically scan it for malicious content Regularly scan every network component and apply security patches in compliance with the corporate security patching and vulnerability management policy

Apply the secure baseline build to every network device and mobile platform.

User education and awareness

Users should understand the risks from malware and the day to day secure processes they need to follow to prevent a malware infection from occurring. The security operating procedures for the corporate desktop should contain the following:

Comply with the removable media policy at all times
Do not open attachments from unsolicited e-mails
Do not click on hyperlinks in unsolicited e-mails
Do not connect any unapproved removable media or any unapproved personally owned device to the corporate network.

For more information consult the BYOD Guidance on www.gov.uk
Report any strange or unexpected system behaviours to the appropriate security team
Maintain an awareness of how to report a security incident

10 Steps To Cyber Security: Monitoring

Detailed cyber security information and advice about monitoring your organisation's ICT activity.

Summary

Monitoring Information and Communications Technologies (ICT) activity allows businesses to better detect attacks and react to them appropriately whilst providing a basis upon which lessons can be learned to improve the overall security of the business. In addition, monitoring the use of ICT systems allows the business to ensure that systems are being used appropriately in accordance with organisational policies. Monitoring is often a key capability needed to comply with security, legal and regulatory requirements.

What is the risk?

Monitoring the organisation's ICT systems provides the business with the means to assess how they are being used by authorised users and if they have been or are being attacked. Without the ability to monitor, an organisation will not be able to:

Detect attacks

Either originating from outside the organisation or attacks as a result of deliberate or accidental insider activity.

React to attacks

So that an appropriate and proportionate response can be taken to prevent or minimise the resultant impact of an attack on the business.

Account for activity

The business will not have a complete understanding of how their ICT systems or information assets are being used or enforce user accountability
Failure to monitor ICT systems and their use for specific business processes could lead to non-compliance with the corporate security policy and legal or regulatory requirements or result in attacks going unnoticed.

How can the risk be managed?

Businesses need to put strategies, policies, systems and processes in place to ensure that they are capable of monitoring their ICT systems and respond appropriately to attacks. A consistent approach to monitoring needs to be adopted across the business that is based on a clear understanding of the risks.

Establish a monitoring strategy and supporting policies

Develop and implement an organisational monitoring strategy and policy based on an assessment of the risks. The strategy should take into account any previous security incidents and attacks and align with the organisation's incident management policies.

Monitor all ICT systems

Ensure that the solution monitors all networks and host

systems (such as clients and servers) potentially through the use of Network and Host Intrusion Detection Systems (NIDS/HIDS) and Prevention Solutions (NIPS/HIPS), supplemented as required by Wireless Intrusion Detection Systems (WIDS). These solutions should provide both signature based capabilities to detect known attacks and heuristic capabilities to detect potentially unknown attacks through new or unusual system behaviour.

Monitor network traffic

The inbound and outbound network traffic traversing network boundaries should be continuously monitored to identify unusual activity or trends that could indicate attacks and the compromise of data. The transfer of sensitive information, particularly large data transfers or unauthorised encrypted traffic should automatically generate a security alert and prompt a follow up investigation. The analysis of network traffic can be a key tool in preventing the loss of data.

Monitor all user activity

The monitoring capability should have the ability to generate audit logs that are capable of identifying unauthorised or accidental input, misuse of technology or data. Critically, it should be able to identify the user, the activity that prompted the alert and the information they were attempting to access.

Test legal compliance

Ensure that the monitoring processes comply with legal or regulatory constraints on the monitoring of user activity.

Fine-tune monitoring systems

Ensure that monitoring systems are fine-tuned appropriately only to collect logs, events and alerts that are relevant in the context of delivering the requirements of the monitoring policy. Inappropriate collection of monitoring information could breach data protection and privacy legislation. It could also be costly in terms storing the audit information and could hinder the efficient detection of real attacks.

Establish a centralised collection and analysis capability

Develop and deploy a centralised capability that can collect and analyse accounting logs and security alerts from ICT systems across the organisation, including user systems, servers, network devices, and including security appliances, systems and applications. Much of this should be automated due to the volume of data involved enabling analysts to quickly identify and investigate anomalies. Ensure that the design and implementation of the centralised solution does not provide an opportunity for attackers to bypass normal network security and access controls.

Ensure there is sufficient storage

Security managers should determine the types of information needed to satisfy the organisation's monitoring policy. Vast quantities of data can be generated and appropriate storage will need to be made available. The organisation will also need to consider the sensitivity of the processed audit logs and any requirement for archiving to satisfy any regulatory or legal requirements.

Provide resilient and synchronised timing

Ensure that the monitoring and analysis of audit logs is supported by a centralised and synchronised timing source that is used across the entire organisation to time-stamp audit logs, alerts and events to support incident response, security investigations and disciplinary or legal action.

Train the security personnel

Ensure that security personnel receive appropriate training on the deployment of monitoring capability and the analysis of security alerts, events and accounting logs.

Align the incident management policies

Ensure that policies and processes are in place to appropriately manage and respond to incidents detected by monitoring solutions.

Conduct a lessons learned review

Ensure that processes are in place to test monitoring capabilities and learn from security incidents and improve the efficiency of the monitoring capability.

10 Steps To Cyber Security: Removable Media Controls

Detailed cyber security information and advice concerning your organisation's removable media controls.

Summary

Failure to control or manage the use of removable media can lead to material financial loss, the theft of information, the introduction of malware and the erosion of business reputation. It is good practice to carry out a risk benefit analysis of the use of removable media and apply appropriate and proportionate security controls, in the context of their business and risk appetite.

What is the risk?

The use of removable media to store or transfer significant amounts of personal and commercially sensitive information is an everyday business process. However, if organisations fail to control and manage the import and export of information from their Information and Communications Technologies (ICT) using removable media they could be exposed to the following risks:

Loss of information

The physical design of removable media can result in it being misplaced or stolen, potentially compromising the confidentiality and availability of the information stored on it

Introduction of malware

The uncontrolled use of removable media will increase the risk from malware if the media can be used on multiple ICT systems

Information leakage

Some media types retain information after user deletion; this could lead to an unauthorised transfer of information between systems

Reputational damage

A loss of sensitive data often attracts media attention which could erode customer confidence in the business

Financial loss

If sensitive information is lost or compromised the organisation could be subjected to financial penalties

How can the risk be managed?

Removable media should only be used to store or transfer information as a last resort, under normal circumstances information should be stored on corporate systems and exchanged using appropriately protected and approved information exchange connections.

Produce corporate policies

Develop and implement policies, processes and solutions to control the use of removable media for the import and export of information.

Limit the use of removable media

Where the use of removable media is unavoidable the business should limit the media types that can be used together with the users, systems and types of information that can be stored or transferred on removable media.

Scan all media for malware

Protect all host systems (clients and servers) with an anti-virus solution that will actively scan for malware when any type of removable media is introduced. The removable media policy should also ensure that any media brought into the organisation is scanned for malicious content by a standalone media scanner before any data transfer takes place.

Audit media holdings regularly

All removable media should be formally issued by the organisation to individuals who will be accountable for its secure use and return for destruction or reuse. Records of holdings and use should be made available for audit purposes.

Encrypt the information held on the media

Where removable media has to be used, the information should be encrypted. The type of encryption should be proportionate to the value of the information and the risks posed to it.

Lock down access to media drives

The secure baseline build should deny access to media drives (including USB drives) by default and only allow access to approved authorised devices.

Monitor systems

The monitoring strategy should include the capability to detect and react to the unauthorised use of removable media within an acceptable time frame.

Actively manage the reuse and disposal of removable media

Where removable media is to be reused or destroyed then appropriate steps should be taken to ensure that previously stored information will not be accessible. The processes will be dependent on the value of the information and the risks posed to it and could range from an approved overwriting process to the physical destruction of the media by an approved third party.

Educate users and maintain their awareness

Ensure that all users are aware of the risks posed to the organisation from the use of removable media and their personal security responsibility for following the corporate removable media security policy.

10 Steps To Cyber Security: Home and Mobile Working

Detailed cyber security information and advice concerning home and mobile working.

Summary

Mobile working offers great business benefit but exposes the organisation to risks that will be challenging to manage. Mobile working extends the corporate security boundary to the user's location. It is advisable for organisations to establish risk-based policies and procedures that cover all types of mobile devices and flexible working if they are to effectively manage the risks. Organisations should also plan for an increase in the number of security incidents and have a strategy in place to manage the loss or compromise of personal and commercially sensitive information and any legal, regulatory or reputational impact that may result.

What is the risk?

Mobile working entails the transit and storage of information assets outside the secure corporate infrastructure, probably across the Internet to devices that may have limited security features. Mobile devices are used in public spaces where there is the risk of oversight and they are also highly vulnerable to theft and loss. If the organisation does not follow good practice security principles and security policies the following risks could be realised:

Loss or theft of the device

Mobile devices are highly vulnerable to being lost or stolen because they are attractive and valuable devices. They are often used in open view in locations that cannot offer the same level of physical security as the organisation's own premises.

Being overlooked

Some users will have to work in public open spaces where they are vulnerable to being observed when working on their mobile device, potentially compromising personal or sensitive commercial information or their user credentials.

Loss of credentials

If user credentials (such as username, password, token) are stored with a device used for remote working and it is lost or stolen, the attacker could potentially compromise the confidentiality, integrity and availability of the organisation's Information and Communications Technologies (ICT).

Tampering

An attacker may attempt to subvert the security controls on the device through the insertion of malicious software or hardware if the device is left unattended. This may allow them to monitor all user activity on the mobile device that could result in the compromise of the confidentiality or integrity of the information.

Compromise of the secure configuration

Without correct training a user may accidentally or intentionally remove or reconfigure a security enforcing control on the mobile device and compromise the secure configuration. This could expose the device to a range of logical attacks that could result in the compromise or loss of any personal or sensitive commercial information the device is storing

How can the risk be managed?

Assess the risks and create a mobile working security policy

Assess the risks to all types of mobile working (including remote working where the device connects to the corporate network infrastructure). The resulting mobile security policy should determine aspects such as the processes for authorising users to work offsite, device acquisition and support, the type of information that can be stored on devices and the minimum procedural security controls. The risks to the corporate network from mobile devices should be assessed and consideration given to an increased level of monitoring on all remote connections and the corporate systems being accessed.

Educate users and maintain their awareness

Without exception, all users should be trained on the secure use of their mobile device for the locations they will be working in. Users should be capable of operating the device securely by following their user specific security procedures at all times, which should as a minimum include direction on: secure storage and management of their user credentials incident reporting environmental awareness (the risks from being overlooked, etc.)

Apply the secure baseline build

All ICT systems should be configured to the secure baseline build including all types of mobile device used by the organisation. Consider integrating the security controls provided in the End User Device guidance (available on www.gov.uk) into the baseline build for mobile devices.

Protect data at rest

Minimise the amount of information stored on a mobile device to only that which is needed to fulfil the business activity that is being delivered when working outside the normal office environment. If the device supports it, encrypt the data at rest.

Protect data in transit

If the user is working remotely the connection back to the corporate network will probably use an untrusted public network such as the Internet. The device and the information exchange should be protected by an appropriately configured Virtual Private Network (VPN).

Review the corporate incident management plans

Mobile working attracts significant risks and security incidents will occur even when users follow the security procedures (such as a forced attack where the user is physically attacked to gain control of the device). The corporate incident management plans should be sufficiently flexible to deal with the range of security incidents that could occur, including the loss or compromise of a device in international locations. Ideally, technical processes should be in place to remotely disable a device that has been lost or at least deny it access to the corporate network.

Appendix B

The form provided in this book is for you to review your own IT system security and resilience, and to assist you to assess the security of your suppliers and particularly any key suppliers.

This scoring process is for your guidance only and you are free to amend the process to fit your business. The reason for providing the forms and the scoring process is to help you. It is easier to amend a document than to be faced with a blank piece of paper.

Supplier Review Process

Below is a detailed explanation of how to use the Supplier Review Form.

Background

Data is a vital part of your business and safe keeping of that data is of utmost importance in order to protect financial interests, maintain regulatory compliance, and to protect company brand and reputation.

Prior to releasing any sensitive Data to an organisation outside of the your company or group (a Supplier), the Supplier should undergo a review of their IT security which may include an analysis of their technical security, operational platforms, procedures and processes, documentation, or any other aspect deemed appropriate dependent upon the Service to be provided.

This document is intended to provide guidance on the categorisation of a Supplier and the review tasks typically carried out at each level. The information within this document is intended to provide guidance more than instruction. Variable factors may alter the severity of a Supplier, Data, Service or risk either up or down.

This document should be read in conjunction with the Supplier Review Criteria which provides guidance on the security questionnaire.

Data Severity.

The volume and type of data that will be provided to, processed or stored by a Supplier can be categorised on a scale of 1 (most critical) to 5 (least critical).

		Data Type			
		Anonymised Data	Basic Personal Data	Sensitive Personal Data	Financial Data
Data Volume	Single or Few	5	4	3	2
	Small Volume	4	3	2	1
	Large Volume	3	2	1	1

Data Severity – Description.

Anonymous Data

- Data which contains no Personally Identifiable Information
- Anonymous data may contain personal reference identifies such as a policy or claim number as access to another data store would be needed in order for such information to be of use or value

Basic Personal Data

- Personally Identifiable Information which is generally available to the public such as name, address, telephone number
- Any other personally associated data other than that considered Sensitive or Financial

Sensitive Personal Data

- Racial or ethnic origin
- Political opinions or religious beliefs
- Trade union membership
- Medical or criminal records
- Sexual orientation or activity

Financial Data

- Any information pertaining to banking or card

details

Data Volume

Single or Few records
    Less than 50 records per month
Small Volume of records
    Less than 1,000 records per month
Large Volume of records
    More than 1,000 records per month

Review Areas

The areas of review typically applicable to a Supplier are:

	No Data or Level 5	Level 4	Level 3	Level 2	Level 1
Questionnaire	No	Yes	Yes	Yes	Yes
Security Testing	No	No	Yes	Yes	Yes
Supporting Documents	No	No	No	Yes	Yes
Site Visit or External Audit	No	No	No	No	Yes
Questionnaire Acceptable Score (inc Web Portal)	N/A	Information Only	100+	110+	120+
Questionnaire Manageable Score	N/A	Information Only	80+	90+	100+
Remedy of Risks	No	No	High	High Medium	High Medium Low

Review Areas – Descriptions

The severity of Data that is to be handled by a Supplier will typically be the dominant factor in determining the extent of review carried out against that Supplier. The key areas of review are:

Questionnaire

> The IT Security standard Supplier review questionnaire provides a high level overview of Supplier procedures, processes and platform security

Security Testing

> Inspection of any platform used in the provision of the Service or the handling of your data

> Testing may be carried out by your IT Security, a contracted external tester, or a Supplier contracted external tester

> Testing typically seeks to verify data and function boundaries

Supporting Documents

> May include technical specifications, network diagrams, data flows, process flows, or any other document deemed appropriate for the Service provided by a Supplier

Site Visit or External Audit

> If the supplier is critical to the continued success of your company, you should consider paying a visit to their site to confirm the answers that you have been given. If you don't have the skills to do this within your organisation, you should consider using the services of an Auditor.

Questionnaire Acceptable Score

> Each questionnaire is rated against a predefined set of acceptable criteria

> A Supplier score above the acceptable score is generally indicative of an overall level of security that is appropriate for the Service provided or the data handled

> Any identified risks or omissions may still be queried

> If no web application or interface is used in the provision of the Service then section 12 may be omitted which will reduce the overall maximum score from 150 to 120, reducing acceptable scores accordingly

Questionnaire Manageable Score

> If a Supplier score falls just below the acceptable score then minor remedial actions or clarifications should be sufficient to increase the score to an acceptable level

If a Supplier score falls significantly below the acceptable score then there are likely to be significant issues or omissions which should be addressed

Where a Supplier score is considered low but the Supplier has demonstrated improvements and a commitment to ongoing improvement then a lower score may be considered acceptable for a period of time

Remedy of Risks

Risks are rated as a combination of the probability of a risk occurring and the severity of impact in the event of that risk occurring

www.ingramcontent.com/pod-product-compliance
Lightning Source LLC
Chambersburg PA
CBHW070856180526
45168CB00005B/1841